D0469378

Violence in a
Post-Conflict Context

*Urban Poor Perceptions
from Guatemala*

Caroline Moser
Cathy McIlwaine

*Latin America and Caribbean Region,
Environmentally and Socially Sustainable Development
Sector Management Unit
The World Bank
Washington, D.C.*

Cover photo: Indian Funeral, Quetzaltenango, Guatemala. Daemrich/The
Image Works.

Caroline Moser is a lead specialist, Social Development, Latin America
and Caribbean Region at the World Bank.

Cathy McIlwaine is lecturer at the Department of Geography, Queen
Mary and Westfield College, London. She was on a one-year sabbatical to
the World Bank to carry out this research.

Library of Congress Cataloging-in-Publication Data has been applied for.

Contents

Boxes

Tables

Figures

Acknowledgments

This study is based on research conducted during April and May 1999, using a participatory urban appraisal methodology. The study is part of a larger initiative within the Environmentally and Socially Sustainable Development Department, Latin America and Caribbean Region, World Bank (the Urban Peace Program) directed by Caroline Moser, Lead Specialist Social Development.

The Swedish International Development Cooperation Agency (SIDA) has provided funding for this program, which also includes a similar study on Colombia. Particular acknowledgment is owed to Eivor Halkjaer for her vision in supporting this very new initiative, as well as to Goren Holmqvist for his continuing support.

In Guatemala, Daniel Selener of the Instituto Internacional de Reconstrucción Rural in Quito was the participatory urban appraisal trainer. The study in the field was organized by Carlos Mendoza of the Centro de Investigaciones Económicas Nacionales (CIEN). The field research was conducted by the authors in collaboration with four teams of researchers from CIEN, Asociación para el Avance de las Ciencias Sociales en Guatemala (AVANCSO), Asociación Mujer Vamos Adelante (AMVA), Fundación de Desarrollo y Servicios Comunitarios (FUNDESCO), and Servicios Profesionales Educativos Integrales (SEPREDI). They included the following members:

AVANCSO

Juan Carlos Martínez Aniorte
María Carina Baquero
José Antonio Gómez
Francisco Reyna Lemus

AMVA

Vilma Ovalle
Zoila Calderón
Tomasa Cortez Guanas
Doris Irene García Posadas
Carmelina Ixay León

FUNDESCO

Alberto Fuentes
Sulma Natalia Gálvez
  de Maldonado
Fernando A. Solares
Brenda Liliana Xulú Guitzol

CIEN/SEPREDI

Carlos Mendoza
Cathy McIlwaine
Lucrecia Rodríguez Illescas
Servio Vanegas

In the World Bank Mission in Guatemala City, Mario Marroquín (Civil Society Representative), José Roberto Lopez-Calix (Resident Representative), and Celeste Peralta provided assistance and support. In identifying research groups Peter Sollis, Patty Ardon, Alfredo Stein, and David Holiday were of great help. In the World Bank's Guatemala Country Management Unit in Washington D.C., Dona Dowsett-Coirolo (Director) and Ian Bannon (Country Economist) provided commitment to the report. World Bank peer reviewers for the study were Shelton Davis (LCSES), Patricia Cleves (SDVCP), Kathy Lindert (LCSHS), and José Roberto Lopez-Calix.

As members of the Urban Peace Program Team, Carolina Ladino and Roddy Brett made important contributions to the data analysis and drafting of this study, while Fiona Clark assisted with the logistics of its publication. Thanks are also due to Jacki Edlund Braun for editing work.

Cathy McIlwaine would like to thank the Department of Geography, Queen Mary and Westfield College, University of London, for granting her a year's leave of absence to pursue this research. Caroline Moser would like to thank Howard Glennister and the Suntory and Toyota Centres for Economic and Related Disciplines (STICERD) for inviting her to be a Visitor at the London School of Economics while writing up the research.

Above all, the authors thank the many people in the nine communities in Guatemala who participated in the research. They not only welcomed us into their lives, shared their time and perceptions, but in some cases took risks in order to contribute to the study. For safety reasons, they must remain anonymous.

Executive Summary

In 1996, the government of Guatemala and the guerrilla army, the Guatemalan National Revolutionary Unity (URNG), signed the final Peace Accords. This ended both the United Nations–monitored peace process and 36 years of internal armed conflict. The civil war caused untold internal and external displacement in the region and the deaths of over 150,000 people, the majority of whom were from indigenous groups. The legacy of conflict, which includes increasing urban violence, social exclusion, and weak levels of social capital, presents challenges for the country's post-conflict peace-building agenda.

As the current government seeks to implement the Peace Accord agreements, the consolidation of democratic governance, the alleviation of the legacy of internal armed conflict, and the strengthening of the rule of law are the primary focus of political analysts and civil society groups alike. The perceptions of violence by people living in poor communities have received less attention. This report addresses this issue by providing the results of a participatory study of violence conducted in low-income, urban communities in Guatemala.

Objectives of the Study

The study documents how people living in poor urban communities in Guatemala perceive violence. Specifically, it identifies the categories of violence affecting poor communities, the costs of different types of violence, the effects of violence on social capital, the interventions employed by people to deal with violence, and the causes and effects of social exclusion.

To describe the relationships that produce and sustain this cycle of violence, and to begin to identify interventions to break it, the study develops a violence–capital–exclusion nexus which is an analytical framework linking different types of violence both to society's capital and to the exclusion of its poor population. To incorporate the rarely heard voices of the poor, the study uses participatory urban appraisal methodology, which emphasizes local knowledge and enables local people to make their own analysis of the problems they face and to identify their own solutions.

Fieldwork was undertaken in nine predominantly low-income "communities" located in six cities and towns. These communities are representative of Guatemala's urban and geographical areas and of the different experiences of violence that took place during the internal armed conflict. These communities, identified by pseudonyms, included four settlements in or near the capital, Guatemala City (Concepción, Nuevo Horizonte, La Merced, and San Jorge, Chinautla); three communities in the western highlands, one of the geographical areas most affected by the civil war (Sacuma in Huehuetenango, Limoncito in San Pedro Sacatepéquez, San Marcos, and Gucumatz in Santa Cruz del Quiché); one settlement in the plantation region of the southern lowlands (El Carmen, Santa Lucía Cotzumalguapa); and a border-town community in the eastern lowlands (Villa Real, Esquipulas). Two of the communities were comprised of mostly indigenous populations—San Jorge, Chinautla, and Gucumatz, Santa Cruz del Quiché—although indigenous people were included in all the other research locations.

Types of Violence

Violence-related problems emerged as the single most important type of problem facing the urban poor. Within this category, social violence was identified as a predominant issue in many communities. Lack of social capital was identified as a problem more often than lack of human capital. Lack of physical capital was identified as less of a problem, and lack of natural capital was perceived as a low-level priority.

Focus groups in the nine communities listed a startling average of 41 different types of violence, which were grouped into three interrelated categories: political, economic, and social. Social violence, including alcohol-related and sexual violence, was cited most often (51 percent of all types of violence), followed by economic violence, pre-eminently gang-related violence and robbery (46 percent), and political violence, such as police abuse (3 percent).

Perceptions of violence varied across cities and demographic groups. Robbery and delinquency emerged as especially important in Limoncito, San Marcos, and El Carmen, Santa Lucía Cotzumalguapa. Intrafamily violence was prevalent in San Jorge, Chinautla, and gang violence was seen as a major problem in Villa Real, Esquipulas. Incidence of political violence was cited most often in Gucumatz, Santa Cruz del Quiché, and Sacuma, Huehuetenango, which are highland towns with large indigenous populations that are particularly affected by the armed conflict.

Perceptions also varied by demographic and ethnic group. Elderly people were most concerned with infrastructure deficiencies, and indigenous elderly people focused on the loss of traditions and the lack of respect among youth. Adult women shared these concerns, but also discussed educational and health concerns and intrafamily violence, while adult men focused on infrastructure and rarely mentioned the latter concerns. Young people were especially concerned with problems related to gangs, particularly with drug-related issues. Young women also emphasized sexual violence and assaults. Children also discussed sexual abuse and problems associated with their schools. In terms of ethnicity, indigenous people tended to stress poverty and discrimination to a greater extent than did the *ladino* population.

The Legacy of Violence in Guatemala

Underlying the contemporary manifestations of violence in Guatemala is the legacy of armed conflict. In the post-conflict con-

text, where political violence has declined and economic and social violence increased, all three types are interrelated. One important issue in this context was the *cultura de silencio* (culture of
silence) that permeated communities, closely linked with fear and
terror of civil war. While indigenous and *ladino* groups were both
affected, indigenous people in particular highlighted continuing
discrimination, especially in terms of widespread poverty and
exclusion, as well as the erosion of indigenous cultures. Another
important issue to emerge was the rape of women, both inside
and outside the home. The alarming preponderance of rape
among all communities had important roots in armed conflict.
During the 1980s rape had been used as a political "tool of war,"
generally against indigenous women. Finally, the war has led to
transformations in household structures, especially an increase
in female-headed households. These were especially common
among displaced indigenous people in the communities in Santa
Lucía Cotzumalguapa and Guatemala City who had fled from
the highlands during the 1980s.

Costs, Causes, and Consequences of Violence

Different types of violence are interrelated in a highly complex
and dynamic way. Social violence within households and families, for instance, may erode social capital, leading young people
to drink, take drugs, and join gangs, which in itself may lead to
economic violence, such as robbery and killing, or to sexual violence, such as rape. Understanding each type of violence is, therefore, critical to understanding the nature of the problems facing
people living in poor communities.

Families, Households, and Social Violence

Intrafamily violence was endemic in the Guatemalan communities and was closely associated with other types of violence. This
was true regardless of ethnicity, income level, or geographical
location with high levels in all communities. Participants identified numerous types of violence perpetrated within the home,
including incest, sexual abuse, and physical abuse. These were

associated with various contingent factors, such as the changing economy, the unemployment rate, alcohol and drug abuse, family disintegration, and issues associated with male *machismo* and female submissiveness.

Intrafamily violence was perceived as undermining how households functioned internally in terms of constructing and maintaining norms, values, and trust. It also led to the erosion of social capital networks between households and reduced the human capital endowments of children and young people. Critically, violence in the home was perceived as leading to violence outside the home.

Violence was perceived as permeating the spectrum of social relations within poor urban communities, with the critical nexus being households and families. With trust in the home severely eroded by violence, children and youth spend long periods of time in the street with their friends. This resulted in young men often looking to the *maras* (gangs) as a source of support and young women engaging in sexual relations at an early age.

Alcohol Consumption and Social Violence

By far the most critical cause of social violence in all communities was alcohol consumption, especially among men. Both legal alcohol (mainly rum and beer) and illegal alcohol (mainly paint thinner and home-made *kusha*) were consumed, the latter mainly by indigenous people. Significantly, acute levels of alcohol consumption were common in all communities with tolerance levels much higher related to drinking than to drug consumption in all communities. While some indigenous groups reported especially high levels of alcohol use linked with trauma and poverty, alcohol abuse was widespread across the communities, regardless of ethnicity.

The most frequently cited causal factors for alcohol abuse were intrafamily violence and conflict, family disintegration, parental example, poverty, and disillusion with employment prospects. Peer pressure and *machismo* also played a part in causing alcohol consumption. The major consequences of alcohol abuse in the home were intrafamily violence and economic hardship, cited in all communities. Outside of the home, economic violence, such as robbery, and sexual violence were perceived as effects of alcohol abuse.

Drug Consumption and Economic Violence

Drug consumption was common particularly among men and members of the *maras* and included a wide range of drugs, such as marijuana, cocaine, including crack. It was perceived as a leading cause of economic violence in all of the communities, as well as a cause of high levels of social violence. However, drug-related problems were few compared to those resulting from alcohol, although they were seen as being integrally related to the problem of the *maras.*

Alcoholism among parents, intrafamily violence, family disintegration, and poverty were frequently cited as causes of drug consumption. Peer pressure and *machismo* within gangs also contributed to consumption. The major consequences of drug consumption included economic violence, such as robbery, and high levels of sexual violence, particularly rape. Drug-related problems also contributed to the generation of fear in the communities, affecting indigenous and *ladino* communities more or less equally.

Maras, Robbers, Delinquents, and Violence

Violence perpetrated by gangs dominated reports of economic violence and included robbery and assault. However, *maras* were also associated with street and gang fighting, as well as sexual violence (predominantly rape). Many considered sexual violence to be the most serious problem associated with the *maras.* The most common members of gangs were young men, although some female-only gangs existed, and male-dominated gangs sometimes had female members. While less widespread, *maras* existed among indigenous populations as well as *ladino. Mara* members perceived their gangs as a positive support structures—important local social organizations that had spread widely in the last decade, largely influenced by young people returning from El Salvador, Honduras, or North America. Although *maras* were associated with robbery and delinquency, robbers and delinquents were also significant actors involved in violence in their own right. While *maras* were involved in economic and social violence, these other groups mainly perpetrated economic violence.

Community-Level Social Institutions and Perverse and Productive Social Capital

Study participants identified 322 social institutions across the nine research communities. These included institutions that benefited the community (productive social capital) and institutions that benefited their members, while hurting the community as a whole (perverse social capital).

Despite the large number of local organizations, all nine communities lacked institutional diversity. The majority were service delivery organizations, with churches the main membership groups. International nongovernmental organizations (NGOs) also played an important role in communities, especially those with predominantly indigenous populations, and were often more trusted than community-based organizations. Cognitive social capital was also very weak in all communities, regardless of the ethnicity of community members. There was notable mistrust and lack of solidarity, with widespread small-scale conflicts in all communities. Underlying this weakness was fear—a legacy of the armed conflict.

State and government institutions, especially the army and the police, were widely distrusted. However, trust in the police varied across communities, depending on whether or not the reformed police force (the National Civil Police, PNC) had been installed. Generally levels of trust were far higher in the new police force than in the preceding police system, and the PNC was cited as responsible for the reduction in economic and social violence in some communities. Linked with this overall mistrust in justice systems and widespread impunity, is the fact that both indigenous and *ladino* community members continually reported the need to take justice into their own hands through social cleansing and lynching.

Community Perceptions of Solutions to Violence

Study participants identified four types of strategies for dealing with violence: avoidance, confrontation, conciliation, and other strategies. Most people responded to violence by keeping silent about it out of powerlessness or fear of retribution. Many changed their mobility patterns, avoiding taking certain routes or simply staying home in the evening.

People in the communities recognized that breaking the continuum of violence requires that a variety of solutions be implemented simultaneously, combining both short-term strategies and longer-term interventions. More than half of the interventions proposed involved creating social capital. Within this category, the promotion of family values and mechanisms to foster trust between neighbors and community members were the most frequently mentioned proposals. Other interventions included improving academic and vocational education as well as drug prevention and sex education programs, and establishing more drug and alcohol rehabilitation centers. Many community members also recommended increasing the resources of community organizations as well as greater police presence in communities. Some endorsed social cleansing, deporting of foreign *mara* leaders, stronger military protection, and longer prison sentences. In general, suggestions were mentioned equally by indigenous and *ladino* focus groups.

Constraints and Recommendations

Despite the signing of the Peace Accords, urban poor communities perceived that violence still pervade their communities. Indeed in some cases they considered the current phase to be worse than the civil war itself. The perceptions of the poor, therefore, can help policymakers in both government and civil society to formulate appropriate violence reduction policies. Local communities identified three interrelated national-level constraints to solving the problem of violence:

- *Extensive fear and distrust.* The legacy of decades of civil war and armed conflict is an extreme level of fear, fre-

quently manifested in a culture of silence. This has resulted
in a lack of social cohesion within communities, distrust
even of neighbors and friends, and associated low levels
of both structural and cognitive social capital.

- *Discrimination and exclusion of the indigenous population.*
  Human rights violations and counterinsurgency policy
  particularly targeted at the indigenous population during
  the civil war, as well as continuing racial and cultural discrimination, has resulted in the persistent exclusion of
  these groups within Guatemalan society. This has exacerbated their levels of fear and social cohesion even in the
  post-conflict context.
- *Lack of trust or confidence in the police and judicial system.* The
  severe lack of confidence in the government's capacity to
  provide adequate police or judicial protection fosters development of alternative informal social cleansing justice
  systems such as lynching. Nevertheless, the new *Policia
  Nacional Civil* is held in much higher regard than the former
  Policia Nacional—with associated lower levels of delinquency, robbery, and violence in communities served by
  the PNC.

Local-level recommendations for reducing violence can be summarized in terms of six priorities:

- *Rebuild trust in the police and judicial system.* Despite partial
  progress to address this issue through, for instance, the
  introduction of the PNC in some areas, fundamental measures are still needed to rebuild trust at the local level if
  informal justice and social cleansing are to be eliminated.
  This includes countrywide introduction of the PNC, along
  with extensive interventions to build their capacity and
  reduce corruption. Fear and distrust on the part of the indigenous population will remain until human rights abuses
  and reconciliation issues are transparently addressed
  through the judicial system.
- *Attack the problem of alcoholism.* The high level of alcohol
  consumption was one of the most important concerns in

all communities. A comprehensive strategy must include prevention through increased public awareness as well as rehabilitation of alcoholics. Implementing such a solution requires collaboration among education, health, social welfare, and other sectors, as well as between the government and NGOs, such as Alcoholics Anonymous, that have long battled the problem.

- *Reduce society's tolerance for intrafamily violence.* All communities acknowledged the high levels of social violence within the home. Dealing with both physical and mental abuse requires a strategy that encompasses both prevention and rehabilitation and can be constructively linked to alcohol-prevention programs. Given the high levels of tolerance in Guatemala for intrafamily violence, a holistic approach, with extensive interagency, media, and NGO collaboration, may help to begin to meet the demand from communities to address this issue so that it includes the needs of women and children alike.

- *Prevent the spread of drug consumption.* To date drug consumption is more concentrated in the capital and has not yet reached epidemic proportions on a nationwide scale. It is, however, a critical concern in most communities. While preventative programs are needed to control the increasing spread of drugs to towns outside the capital, larger urban areas also require rehabilitation programs. This requires collaboration across sectors in the government, as well as between the government and NGOs.

- *Transform* maras *from perverse to productive social organizations.* Given the growing preoccupation with *maras* in poor communities, and the distinctions among them—ranging from highly violent gangs to support structures for local youth—innovative inclusive programs could involve young people themselves in overcoming violence-related problems. Such interventions could include drug prevention, issues of self-esteem, as well as skills-training to access local employment opportunities. To dissolve the highly violent gangs in larger urban areas may require both punitive and rehabilitative initiatives.

- *Develop mechanisms to build sustainable community-based membership organizations.* Rebuilding the fabric of local communities and their social organizations whose trust and cohesion have been shattered by the civil war, presents particular challenges requiring community consultation. Locally based organizations that meet perceived needs are more likely to be sustainable. For instance, to address the severe problem of the lack of childcare among working parents—currently blamed for many problems—local organizations for the care and support of both children and youth, run by women and men in the community, might be an appropriate initiative that serves both an immediate need while also rebuilding local trust and social capital.

People living in poor urban communities recognize that in this post-conflict context the problem of violence is so complex that it requires cross-sector solutions. They also recognize that local ownership is crucial if the sense of fear, powerlessness, and lack of trust is to be overcome. Given the conventional sector divisions in government ministries and NGOs alike, developing such solutions is likely to prove challenging.

1
Introduction

G uatemala has long been one of the most violent societies in Central America. The conflict has been rooted in centuries of exclusion and inequality, largely along racial divisions—between *ladino* and indigenous populations.[1] The recent civil war involved extreme and brutal levels of political violence, principally affecting the indigenous population. Despite the Peace Accords signed between the government and the Guatemalan National Revolutionary Unity (URNG) in 1996, which ended most of the political violence, generalized violence has increased. With homicide rates of 34 per 100,000 inhabitants, Guatemala is currently considered the most violent country in Central America (CIEN 1998:1). Figures from the Programa de Naciones Unidas para el Desarrollo (PNUD) compound these findings. High homicide rates existed in 1996 in the departments of Escuintla (16.5 per 10,000 inhabitants), Izabal (12.7 per 10,000 inhabitants), Jutiapa (11.4 per 10,000 inhabitants), Santa Rosa (11.1 per 10,000 inhabitants), and Guatemala (10.1 per 10,000 inhabitants). As noted by the PNUD, these departments have predominantly *ladino* populations, a marked absence of indigenous people, and, overall, possess relatively high levels of human development (PNUD 1998:149).

In the post-conflict context following the Peace Accords, Guatemalans recognize the need to prioritize generalized crime and violence as a major concern. The political violence perpetrated during the civil war was concentrated in the rural, northwestern, and north central departments of the country, in areas dominated by indigenous populations. Today, however, rates of violent crime are soaring throughout the country, especially in urban areas previously immune from the worst ravages of the war. According to violence trends cited by the PNUD, the number of violent deaths increased from 2,699 in 1992, to 3,657 in 1995, although the figure dropped slightly to 3,281 in 1996 (PNUD 1998:148). Furthermore, the total number of crimes committed in Guatemala rose dramatically from 11,711 in 1992, to 22,742 in 1995, again decreasing only slightly in 1996 to 19,094 (PNUD 1998:148). Of particular significance was a marked increase in the number of kidnappings, in general executed in Guatemala City, from 162 in 1995, to 182 in 1996 (PNUD 1998:148). Finally, between 1994 and 1996, registered non-natural deaths increased from 1,409 to 1,451, peaking in 1995 at 1,687. These figures signify that Guatemala has become a substantially more violent country since the end of the internal armed conflict.

As violence continues to affect the daily lives of Guatemalan citizens, two major concerns have emerged; first, that high levels of violence may undermine current economic stability and constrain economic growth; second, that the Peace Accords may be jeopardized unless violence and crime are addressed as priority issues (CIEN 1998; PNUD 1998; World Bank 1998). Underlying both these issues is the need to build sustainable peace by focusing on exclusion, poverty, and inequality. While these lie at the roots of the conflict, the civil war has tended only to exacerbate them further.

Such issues were central to the World Bank's 1998 Country Assistance Strategy (CAS), which identified four main themes: (a) building social cohesion and strengthening participatory processes, (b) reducing poverty, (c) improving economic management to maintain stability and foster growth, and (d) modernizing the public sector to make it more efficient (World Bank 1998:i-ii).

Objectives and Research Framework of the Study

With the implementation of the Peace Accords, civil society groups have also continued to focus on human rights violations of the peace process in rural areas (Palencia Prado 1996; MINUGUA 1998a, 1998b; ODHAG 1998, 1998). In contrast, the business community has increasingly become preoccupied with economic crime, kidnapping, and robbery (IEPADES 1998). Less well known, however, are the perceptions of violence among poor communities. To address this issue, the following report provides the results of a study of violence conducted in nine urban low-income communities in Guatemala. The study was undertaken as part of the World Bank's contribution to developing operational interventions to build social cohesion and reduce poverty in Guatemala.

The objective of the study is to document violence in Guatemala as perceived by poor urban communities themselves in terms of the following four questions:

- *What categories of violence affect poor communities?* Is it the crime and robbery that dominate the newspapers and preoccupy the politicians or the human rights violations that concern civil society groups? Or are other types of violence also important to poor communities? Building on the work of Guatemalan violence experts and the World Bank's Urban Peace Program (World Bank 1998; Moser and Shrader 1999), the study distinguishes among political, economic, and social violence—identifying each in terms of a particular type of power that consciously or unconsciously uses that violence to gain or maintain itself.

- *What are costs of the different types of violence?* Does violence exact a financial or psychological burden on poor communities, households, and individuals? The study distinguishes four types of capital: physical, human, natural, and social, each with a number of associated assets that violence can erode. Assessing the impacts of violence on a country's capital and its associated stocks of assets facilitates a more comprehensive understanding of the true price of violence.

- *Does violence erode or foster social capital?* Does "social capital for some" imply "social exclusion for others"? (Harriss and De Renzio 1997:926). Not only may social capital generate negative outcomes, but social capital itself may be generated by activities that do not serve the public good. In examining this issue the study makes a distinction between productive (positive) and unproductive (perverse) social capital (Rubio 1997).

- *Is violence the cause or consequence of exclusion?* The complex relationship between violence and poverty has been widely debated. However, social exclusion—the process through which individuals or groups are excluded from full participation in the society in which they live—may be a more useful concept because it involves a more dynamic and multidimensional conceptualization of deprivation. The study thus seeks to identify the causal linkages between violence and exclusion.

- *The violence–capital–exclusion nexus.* How best can the interrelationship among these three multi-layered phenomena of categories, costs, and causes and consequences of violence be analyzed? To identify the relationships that produce and sustain violence in poor urban communities in Guatemala and to begin to identify interventions to break this cycle, the study develops a violence–capital–exclusion nexus (figure 1.1). This analytical framework links different types of violence to both society's capital and the exclusion of its poor population.

Figure 1.1   Framework for analysis: violence–capital–exclusion

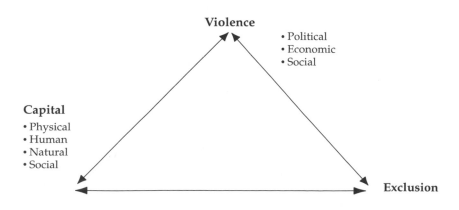

The Participatory Methodology and its Implications for Policy Recommendations

Like poverty, violence can be measured in different ways (see Baulch 1996; Moser 1998). Both poverty and violence can be measured objectively using large, random-sample household surveys that use measures of income or consumption as proxies for the variable being measured (Ravaillon 1992). Both can also be understood subjectively using participatory assessments that collect data on multiple indicators that emerge out of the complex and diverse local realities in which the poor live (Chambers 1992, 1995).

Statistical and political analyses of post-conflict violence in Guatemala, though scarce, do exist (IEPADES 1998; Palma 1998). To complement those findings with the rarely heard voices of the poor, this study uses a participatory urban appraisal methodology. This approach emphasizes local knowledge and enables local people to make their own appraisals, analyses, and plans.[2] Its iterative approach to research is suitable for the investigation of the complex causal relationships that affect violence (Moser and McIlwaine 1999). The reliability of the findings is increased through triangulation—the use of a variety of techniques and sources to investigate the same issues and verify results. Qualitative research such as this study, which relies on in-depth investigation of a small number of communities, also uses purposive rather than random sampling. This means selecting communities that are considered representative of the issue under investigation and conducting a participatory urban appraisal with sufficient groups to be broadly representative of each community (see annex A for a summary of participatory urban appraisal techniques).

Participatory urban appraisal involves an extensive number of different tools (see annex A). The most important ones used in the current study are listings that provided the basis for the quantitative data analysis, causal impact diagrams that analyzed the causes and effects of particular issues, and the institutional mapping diagrams that allowed the identification of social institutions perceived as important within communities. All participatory urban appraisal tools were implemented in focus groups facilitated by two researchers and comprising between 2 and 20 people (occasionally they were conducted with one person).

The primary aim of participatory urban appraisal is to allow the people to express their own ideas and perceptions in an inductive manner. Therefore, in the focus groups people were encouraged to design the diagrams and provide the associated text themselves. This process often is referred to as "handing over the stick" (in the urban Guatemalan context it usually involves pens and pencils). The rationale behind this methodology is the transfer of power from the researcher to the researched (Chambers 1995). Consequently, all the diagrams reproduced in this document were drawn by people in the communities themselves and use their language.[3]

The study describes community perceptions of the causes, costs, and consequences of violence and identifies local perceptions of potential solutions to the problems described. Whether perception data can legitimately be used to influence or define violence reduction policies or strategies is currently an issue of debate. The Bank's recently completed report "Global Synthesis: Consultations with the Poor" (Narayan and others 1999) that is used in the latest *World Development Report 2000/2001*, and its endorsement by Bank President James Wolfensohn in his 1999 annual meeting address, have certainly given a measure of legitimacy to this approach in international agencies.

During the past decade several innovative interventions have been proposed to reduce violence (table 1.1). All of the approaches reflect different solutions, although in general there has been a shift away from the control of violence toward violence prevention, and most recently toward rebuilding social capital.

By presenting bottom-up solutions to violence, this study aims to contribute to the search for sustainable solutions. The solutions recommended are those that local communities themselves perceive as appropriate. The approach adopted here, therefore, is one of a number of approaches that can guide policymakers concerned with reducing violence.

Table 1.1 Different policy approaches to violence intervention

Approach	Objective	Category of violence addressed	Policy/planning intervention	Limitations
Criminal justice	Violence deterrence and control through higher arrest and conviction rates and more severe punishment	Economic	Top-down strengthening of judicial, penal, and police systems and their associated institutions	Limited applicability to situations of political and social violence; success highly dependent on enforcement
Public health	Violence prevention through the reduction of individual risk factors	Economic Social	Top-down surveillance; risk factor identification; resultant behavior modification; scaling up of successful interventions	Almost exclusive focus on individual; often imposed top-down; highly sensitive to quality of surveillance data; limitations in indicators
Conflict transformation	Achieving nonviolent resolution of conflict through negotiated terms between conflicting parties	Political Social	Negotiations to ensure conflict reduction between different social actors—often using third party mediation. May be top-down or bottom-up	Often long term in its impact; often faces challenges in bringing parties to the table and in mediating conflict
Human rights	Legal enforcement of human rights and documentation of abuses by states, and other social actors	Political Social	Top-down legal enforcement reinforced by bottom-up popular participation and NGO lobbying	Legalistic framework often difficult to enforce in a context of lawlessness, corruption, and impunity; documentation of abuse sometimes dangerous
Social capital	Building social capital to reduce violence in both informal and formal social institutions, such as families, community organizations, and the judiciary	Political Economic Social	Bottom-up participatory appraisal of violence; institutional mapping to address problems; community participation in violence-reduction measures	Less well articulated than other approaches; fewer indicators developed

Problems Associated with Using a Participatory Urban Appraisal to Study Violence

Determining perceptions of violence in communities deeply affected by violence is difficult for several reasons. The first and by far the most important constraint in all communities was the culture of silence (*cultura de silencio*), which made people reluctant to discuss violence directly or indirectly. This fundamentally affected the research project, given the transitional post-conflict Guatemalan context. This culture of silence was most evident in communities that were directly affected by the civil war and had experienced threats and even killings of community members. It was also particularly pronounced among the indigenous population (see chapter 3). However, as demonstrated by the relatively recent assassination of Monsenor Juan Gerardi Conadera, such fear is indeed highly valid in all communities.[4] Indeed, fear was widespread regardless of ethnicity in all the communities, despite slightly stronger concern expressed by indigenous groups.

Second, intrafamily violence is a highly sensitive issue. Young people were often more willing to discuss the issue than older people, and women were more likely to raise the issue than men. The problem of alcohol abuse, a major cause of intrafamily violence, was often used as a conduit to discuss violence in the home.

To ensure the safety of the people who participated in the study and prevent retribution, the researchers changed the names of all study participants and communities.[5] To ensure the researchers' safety and help negotiate with gatekeepers, the research teams included people with guaranteed access to the communities, usually because they had previously worked there.

Description of Researchers and Categorization of Communities Studied

In the selection of research teams, the overall aim was to identify an academic team (AVANCSO), a women's NGO (AMVA), a community development NGO (FUNDESCO), and NGOs working at the national level (CIEN/SEPREDI). The team members were drawn from a diversity of backgrounds, ranging from formally trained researchers (AVANCSO) to beneficiaries of community projects (FUNDESCO). Of a total of 16 researchers, nine were female and seven were male. Both FUNDESCO and AMVA had indigenous researchers—with four indigenous women in total. Furthermore, AVANCSO researchers in particular were especially sensitive to indigenous issues, given their long history of research on human rights and exclusion issues.

Fieldwork was undertaken in nine predominantly low-income settlements or communities, located in six cities and towns that are broadly representative of Guatemala's urban areas (table 1.2). The communities selected reflect coverage of different geographical areas of the country as well as prevalence of different types of violence and varying experiences of the internal armed conflict. For instance, effort was made to work in the western highlands, the southern lowlands, and the eastern lowlands, as well as the capital region. This included localities directly affected by the conflict (Santa Cruz del Quiché, San Marcos, and Huehuetenango), as well as indirectly (Santa Lucía Cotzumalguapa) and a community relatively untouched (Esquipulas).

While an effort was made to include a range of different ethnic groups by location, this was not the primary aim of the research. Furthermore, given that the research was on urban communities, the proportion of indigenous groups included was lower than the national average. Nonetheless, two communities were predominantly indigenous (Santa Cruz del Quiché and Chinautla), and many indigenous people were included in the research in other communities (see chapter 2).

In collaboration with the local research teams, the study used a number of indicators to identify predominantly urban poor communities: lack of legal land tenure, limited access to basic urban services, as well as the detailed local knowledge of researchers. In addition, according to the PNUD (1998), the majority of the departments included in the research were identified as demonstrating extremely high levels of social exclusion (with the only exceptions being Guatemala City and Escuintla).

The nine research communities can be categorized into four main regional areas. First is the "capital city and towns in central Guatemala," which refers to Guatemala City and its surround-

Table 1.2 Characteristics of research communities

Selection criteria	Community pseudonyms								
	Concepción	Nuevo Horizonte	La Merced	San Jorge	Sacuma	Limoncito	Gucumatz	El Carmen	Villa Real
City	Guatemala City	Guatemala City	Guatemala City	Chinautla	Huehuetenango	San Pedro Sacatepéquez, San Marcos	Santa Cruz del Quiché	Santa Lucía Cotzumalguapa	Esquipulas
Administrative status and spatial location	Capital city in central Guatemala	Capital city in central Guatemala	Capital city in central Guatemala	Small town in central Guatemala	Departmental capital in western highlands	Departmental capital in western highlands	Departmental capital in western highlands	Town in southern lowlands	Border town in eastern lowlands
Socioeconomic status	Poor	Poor	Poor	Poor	Poor	Poor and middle-income	Poor and middle-income	Poor	Poor
Intra-city location	Central urban	Peri-urban	Peri-urban	Peri-urban	Peri-urban	Central urban	Central urban	Peri-urban	Central urban
Date of establishment	1979	1983	1983	Pre-Colombian	1969	1940	Pre-Colombian	1820	1980
Form of establishment	Land invasion	Land invasion	Land invasion	Historic community	Urban development	Urban development	Historic community	Urban development	Urban development
Ethnic composition	Predominantly *ladino*	Predominantly *ladino*	Predominantly *ladino*	Predominantly indigenous *ladino*	Predominantly *ladino*	Predominantly *ladino*	Predominantly indigenous	Predominantly *ladino*	Predominantly *ladino*

ing area. In Guatemala City the researchers undertook fieldwork in Concepción, Nuevo Horizonte, and La Merced, as well as in San Jorge, Chinautla (a small town in central Guatemala approximately 12 kilometers north of the capital city). While these are broadly similar communities, they also have important differences.

All communities in or near the capital are vulnerable to environmental change, given their precarious location near rivers, roads, and ravines. In particular, San Jorge, Chinautla, was vulnerable to erosion and increasing levels of pollution that have affected nearby rivers. Concepción, in zone six of the capital, was formed several years after the earthquake of 1976, when families invaded lands owned by a *finca* (large farm). Residents are, however, still engaged in the process of trying to secure legal title to the land. Nuevo Horizonte and La Merced, both in zone 13, were formed toward the end of 1983 when residents initiated land invasions. Most residents now own the titles to their land. The populations in all three communities, while predominantly *ladino*, except for San Jorge, in many cases originate from departments affected by the internal armed conflict, a major cause of displacement to the capital (see chapter 3). Compared with Nuevo Horizonte and La Merced, where problems with drainage and sanitation are particularly pervasive, residents in Concepción enjoy a comparatively high level of public services. This includes the supply of potable water, electricity, and drainage systems to 100 percent, and public telephone service to 70 percent of the houses in Concepción. A further salient point of comparison is the historically high level of effective organization and community mobilization in the community of Nuevo Horizonte that originated with the invasion of land in 1983.

In contrast to the communities located within the capital, San Jorge, Chinautla, is an indigenous Maya-Pocomam community founded prior to the colonial epoch. Residents have managed to maintain their cultural traditions, customs, and language despite pressures caused by proximity to the capital and high levels of poverty. One manifestation of this is the maintenance of the *cofradía* system,[6] which continues to generate a certain level of cohesion and organization in the community. The predominantly indigenous population does not enjoy substantial levels of public services such as access to water and electricity.

The second urban category, "departmental capitals in the western highlands," is a region populated predominantly by indigenous people and one of the geographical areas most affected by the internal armed conflict, and in particular by the military's counterinsurgency project. This category of communities includes Sacuma in Huehuetenango, Limoncito in San Pedro Sacatepéquez, San Marcos, and Gucumatz in Santa Cruz del Quiché.

Gucumatz predates the colonial period and is located in the ancient capital city of the Maya-Quiché, renamed Santa Cruz del Quiché by the Spanish. In recent years the department and its capital, both predominantly indigenous in population, were the sites of popular, church, and guerrilla mobilizations and, consequently, were subject to acute state-sponsored violence. This has left a legacy of community violence and distrust. A high incidence of mobilization continues with human rights organizations and evangelical sects. In contrast, Sacuma, founded in 1969 with a predominantly *ladino* population, is reputed to be the most dangerous and violent *colonia* (neighborhood) in the departmental capital of Huehuetenango. Its political history is similar to that of El Quiché, although its common border with Mexico has meant an increased incidence of black market activity and illegal migration activity (it is used as a route to the United States). As in Santa Cruz del Quiché, the legacy of the internal armed conflict is also evident in the lack of confidence in the judicial system. However, in Huehuetenango this has resulted in a relatively high occurrence of community-led lynchings (see chapter 3). Limoncito, San Pedro Sacatepéquez, San Marcos,[7] was founded in 1940. The predominantly *ladino* residents and minority indigenous (Maya-Mam) population, who have historically come from rural municipalities throughout the department, engage in a variety of economic enterprises. The community is dominated by small-scale, home-based enterprises such as weaving knitted sweaters using knitting machines. These enterprises supply companies in the capital, which, in turn, often supply foreign *maquilas* (world market factories). The department of San Marcos and its capital were less affected by the internal armed conflict than the other two communities and, given their age, are served by adequate public services, yet as a town, San Marcos is one of the poorest in the country and in the department.

The third urban category is "town in the southern lowlands" with fieldwork undertaken in El Carmen, Santa Lucía Cotzumalguapa. A predominantly *ladino* community, El Carmen was formed around 1820. The town itself is located between the highlands and the coastal plains in the Boca Costa area. This region is characterized by plantation agriculture, especially sugar cultivation. The population increased dramatically during two historical flash points, first in 1972 and again in 1982, mainly as a result of displacement caused by economic migration and the internal armed conflict. This has led to an increase in indigenous groups, especially from Quiché, from where most fled (see chapter 3). The community is relatively well serviced in terms of infrastructure, given its age.

The final urban category is "town in the eastern lowlands" with fieldwork conducted in Villa Real, Esquipulas, founded in 1980. The town of Esquipulas shares borders with Honduras and El Salvador, which has had a significant impact on the community: 20 percent of residents originate from these countries, which themselves suffer severe gang-related problems. Furthermore, the incidence of black market activity is also high. Located on the banks of a river, the community, although well-consolidated, is also subject to annual flooding.

Notes

1. The term *ladino* describes the Guatemalan hispanicized (or *mestizo*) population, descended from Spanish-indigenous origins. The *ladinos* constitute approximately 40 percent of the Guatemalan population, the remainder being made up of 23 indigenous ethnic groups, the largest of which is the Maya (with 21 distinct ethnic groups).

2. Development practitioners use participatory urban appraisal as a research tool for sharing local people's knowledge and perceptions with outsiders. Chambers (1994a, 1994b, 1994c) provides comprehensive detailed reviews of the participatory rural appraisal approach. The techniques used in that methodology are also applicable in urban settings and are used here.

The World Bank's *Participation Sourcebook* includes participatory appraisals as one of the techniques currently being integrated into the Bank's operational work (World Bank 1995). The methodology has already been incorporated into several recent Bank studies, including country poverty assessments in Ghana, South Africa, and Zambia. The first study on urban poverty and violence using this methodology was undertaken in Jamaica in 1996 (Moser and Holland 1997) and more recently in Colombia (Moser and McIlwaine 2000).

3. For both translation and production purposes, the diagrams have been transferred into computerized form.

4. One of the most comprehensive analyses of political violence is the Catholic Church's Interdiocesan Project for the Recuperation of Historical Memory in Guatemala *(Recuperación de la Memoria Histórica* REMHI) (ODHAG 1998). Conducted by the Office of Human Rights of the Archdiocese of Guatemala, and based on oral testimonies, the report documented 55,021 cases of brutal atrocities, of which 79.2 percent was attributed to the Guatemalan military. While it concentrates on the past, it also informs the present through highlighting how the legacy of the war permeates contemporary patterns of violence. The assassination of the project's director, Monsenor Juan Gerardi Conadera, 56 hours after the findings were made public in April 1998, highlight the fragility of the Peace Accords.

5. One of the participatory urban appraisal ground rules is ownership of visual outputs through named acknowledgment. Given the nature of the issue being studied, however, anonymity was considered essential.

6. This is a hierarchical religious brotherhood based on kinship and age-grade ties between families and residents.

7. The areas of San Pedro Sacatepéquez and San Marcos border each other and, while the community of Limoncito was located in San Pedro Sacatepéquez, its administrative base was in the city of San Marcos. For this reason, hereafter, the geographical location of Limoncito is referred to as San Marcos.

2

Summary Findings: Perceptions of General Problems and Violence

Rather than ask community members specifically about violence, the participatory urban appraisals first focused on people's perceptions of the main problems affecting them and their community. In this way, it did not assume that violence would necessarily be an important issue in people's daily lives.

Characteristics of Focus Groups

In all nine communities a total of approximately 1,860 people were involved in focus group discussions. Broadly equal proportions of women and men were included, either in male- and female-only groups or mixed sessions. The researchers made efforts to include all ages in various focus groups, usually classified as elderly, adult, adolescent, and children. Ethnically, approximately 30 percent of all community members included were of indigenous origin.[1] As far as possible, the diagrams throughout the text reflect this diversity of gender, age, and ethnicity.[2]

Perceptions of Problems in Poor Urban Communities

Violence was the single most frequently cited problem facing the urban poor in the nine urban poor communities (table 2.1). Re-

26

**Table 2.1   Frequency listings of types of problems identified
in nine urban communities**

Type of problem	Percentage of total problems cited
Violence	48
Lack of physical capital	25
Lack of social capital	10
Lack of human capital	9
Lack of natural capital	8
Total	**100**

Source: 199 focus group listings of problems.

spondents in focus groups identified 13 different types of violence-related problems, with theft and gangs leading the list. Theft
and robbery represented over one-fifth of all violence problems
(21 percent) with gangs representing just under one-fifth (19 percent) (annex B, table B.1). It is important to emphasize that these
two problems were invariably discussed as interlinked, with gang
members cited as major perpetrators of robbery (see chapter 7).

Important variations exist in perceptions of violence among
different communities. For instance, Sacuma, Huehuetenango,
had the highest proportion of violence problems (60 percent of
the total), which community members blamed on the city's proximity to the Mexican border and its attraction for other Central
Americans. In contrast, in San Jorge, Chinautla, violence represented only one-third of the problems identified. San Jorge is a
mainly indigenous Maya-Pocomam community in a small town
established in pre-Colombian times north of Guatemala City. Here
problems of violence were perceived to gradually spread geographically from the capital itself.

Ranking of Perceived Problems in Poor Urban Communities

Focus groups ranked problems according to their importance. In
most communities problems linked with violence were most fre-

quently cited and prioritized as most important. Problems linked with gang violence were ranked as important in most settlements such as Concepción, Nuevo Horizonte, and La Merced in Guatemala City; Limoncito, San Marcos; and San Jorge, Chinautla. Figure 2.1 highlights how violence often dominated both the listings and prioritization of general problems. Particularly significant here is that children as young as ten years of age ranked death, rape, and kidnappings as the most important problems in their community. Indeed, the only problems not associated with violence were pollution and AIDS (figure 2.1).

Lack of Physical Capital

Lack of physical capital represented one quarter of all problems identified in communities (table 2.1). Within this category, deficiencies in public services were mentioned most frequently (13 percent). These services included sanitation facilities, especially the lack of adequate drainage systems that plagued Nuevo

Figure 2.1 "Onion" diagram ranking types of general problems in Sacuma, Huehuetenango, drawn by four children (aged 10–13)

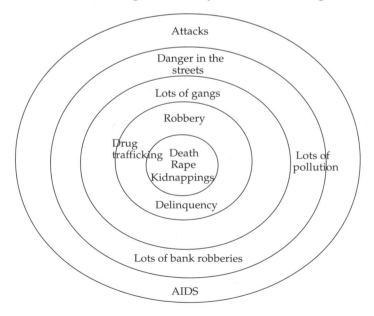

Horizonte and La Merced in Guatemala City and Villa Real, Esquipulas. In other cases, the physical capital category referred to lack, or irregularity of, drinking water supply, in terms of quality and availability—a problem identified most frequently in four of the communities. It also included lack of rubbish collection, which was a particular problem in San Jorge, Chinautla (annex B, table B.1).

Besides lack of urban services, the issues of poverty were identified in all communities, although this was particularly significant in El Carmen, Santa Lucía Cotzumalguapa, and La Merced, Guatemala City. This was viewed as more important than unemployment, which was not perceived as a substantive problem in the communities. In El Carmen, however, poor working conditions rather than lack of work per se were cited as a frequent problem This was linked with the plantation economy that provided seasonal, irregular employment. Indigenous groups, in particular, complained of poverty and poor working conditions.

Lack of Social Capital

Lack of social capital (10 percent) was identified more frequently than lack of human capital as a problem (see table 2.1). This lack of social capital referred to mistrust and lack of cooperation within the community. These were associated with widely held lack of understanding and unity, lack of communication between people, and the perception that "people don't care." Of particular importance for indigenous people was the loss of traditions. This usually referred to a decline in wearing traditional dress (traje), as well as loss of indigenous language. For others the loss of traditional values related to lack of respect for the elderly. Discrimination also emerged as a problem in a number of communities, again related mainly with indigenous peoples (see chapter 3).

Lack of Human Capital

Lack of human capital emerged in all communities (9 percent) (table 2.1). Important problems relating to education included the lack of services in primary schools, the poor quality of teaching

Figure 2.2 Child's drawing of fear in Concepción, Guatemala City

provided, and the lack of secondary-level educational establishments. Health problems were linked to the dearth of health facilities and their high cost, as well as the prevalence of diseases among local families. These problems were often associated with the lack of urban services.

Lack of Natural Capital

Members of communities cited problems relating to natural capital particularly where rivers ran through or adjacent to the settlement (Concepción, Guatemala City; Sacuma, Huehuetenango, Villa Real, Esquipulas; and San Jorge, Chinautla). Invariably people complained of the bad smell and associated health hazards—such as mosquitoes—of rivers as well as the lack of protective walls to prevent flooding. Indeed, flooding was a major problem in all these communities in the rainy season.

Perceptions of Problems by Demographic Group and Ethnicity

Focus groups highlighted problems that reflected their specific needs. These were differentiated mainly by gender, age, and ethnicity. Elderly women and men were more likely to discuss infrastructure deficiencies than other types of problems, especially those related to violence. Elderly women in particular also focused on the loss of traditions and the lack of respect among youth in contemporary society. Adult women shared most of the concerns of the elderly, but also identified education and health problems as priorities. They were also more likely to discuss intrafamily violence and its links to alcohol abuse. Adult men rarely mentioned such issues, since they tended to be the perpetrators, and focused instead on infrastructure, especially deficient drainage systems.

Adolescents of both genders were the most likely to identify problems related to gangs. They often linked this with drug consumption, citing the latter as a growing problem for young people. This affected male youth in particular. Young women were more likely to discuss sexual violence and assaults, both as a result of drug consumption and of alcohol abuse. Children were also keenly aware of violence issues, although they often discussed problems associated with their schools, such as the violence of teachers.

The various indigenous groups included in the focus groups across the communities were most likely to identify poverty as a problem, as well as various social capital problems such as discrimination. Their perceptions of violence coincided broadly with those of the *ladino* population, except in relation to human rights abuses, which were only identified in Gucumatz, Santa Cruz del Quiché—a predominantly indigenous community (see chapter 3).

Perceptions of Violence in Poor Urban Communities

Focus groups in the nine communities listed an alarming average of 41 different types of violence, with one community (Sacuma, Huehuetenango) distinguishing 70 different types.

Types of violence ranged from gangs and drugs violence, to lynchings and assassinations, as well as violence within the home. Figure 2.3 reveals the types of perceived violence faced by people in La Merced, Guatemala City, according to a young woman; she perceived robbery, gangs, rape, violence within the home, activities of the local mafias, and violence linked with drug addicts as the main types.

The majority of listings referred to types of violence (*violencias*), although in some cases a more locally acceptable term was dangers (*peligros*). *Peligros* referred to all types of violence and insecurity affecting local communities, in contrast to *violencias*, which were often perceived as political violence and conflict associated with the civil war. Some focus groups qualified the term, listing its constituent parts. Table 2.2 shows how a group of young men distinguished between the two types and how they were manifested at the individual, group, community, and city levels. Generally, danger denoted the threat of force, whereas violence denoted the act itself.

Figure 2.3 Flow diagram of types of violence facing La Merced, Guatemala City (prepared by a 16-year-old woman)

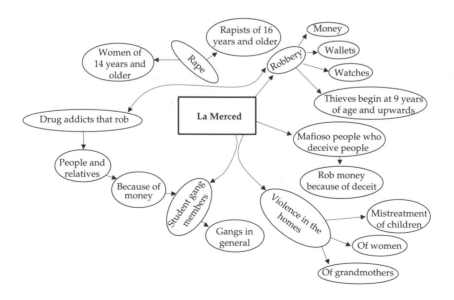

Table 2.2   Types of violence and danger in Villa Real,
Esquipulas (identified by a group of three young men
aged 14–17)

Sphere of influence	Types of danger	Types of violence
Individual	People who kill Drunk people	Parents who hit their children Children in prostitution Adults who abuse children
Group	Gangs Arms Inhalants	Drugged people who can kill

Community	People from other
	  places who come
	  with negative
	  attitudes
		Drunk people who push
		  people over
		People who mistreat others
		  physically and verbally

City	Some people that
	  carry arms
	Adolescents carrying
	  arms
	Gangs going out at
	  night
		Child abuse
		Gangs that abuse people
		Assaults

Differences Among Economic, Social, and Political Violence

Listings of violence were grouped together under three rubrics:
political, economic, and social. Social violence was disaggregated
into violence within the home, violence outside the home, and
either (to categorize rape when it was not clear where it occurred).
These types of violence represent a continuum of categories that
overlap and are not mutually exclusive.[3]

Both social and economic violence were more frequently mentioned than political violence across all nine communities, in
broadly equal proportions. However, social violence was slightly
more dominant, representing exactly half of all types of violence

Table 2.3   Types of violence faced by nine urban communities

Types of violence	Percentage of total types of violence cited
Economic	46
Social	50
Inside the home	14
Outside the home	28
Inside-outside the home	8
Political	3
Total	100

(50 percent). Economic violence represented just under a half at 46 percent nationally, while political violence constituted only 3 percent (table 2.3).[4]

Among communities, the frequency of violence reflects context-specific complexities. In Limoncito, San Marcos, economic rather than social violence was the most prevalent (59 percent), with one of the higher levels of robbery, assaults, and delinquency of the nine communities. However, levels of robbery and assaults were highest in El Carmen, Santa Lucía Cotzumalguapa, because of the instability of the local plantation economy. In contrast, in San Jorge, Chinautla, social violence represented three-quarters of all types of violence (75 percent), with the highest incidence of intrafamily violence nationally (29 percent) (annex C, table C.1).

Political violence was identified in seven of the nine communities. It was most frequently cited in Gucumatz, Santa Cruz del Quiché (8 percent) and in Sacuma, Huehuetenango (7 percent) — both areas in the indigenous highland region that was particularly affected by the civil conflict and where the majority of massacres took place during the war (REMHI 1998). These low proportions are not surprising given the official cessation of the civil conflict in 1996, as well as the culture of silence that surrounds the issue (see chapter 3).

Ranking Types of Violence

As with discussions of general problems affecting communities, focus groups also identified the most serious types of violence through ranking or prioritization. *Mara* or gang issues were the most commonly prioritized as important in five of the nine communities: Nuevo Horizonte and La Merced, Guatemala City; San Jorge, Chinautla; Limoncito, San Marcos; and El Carmen, Santa Lucía Cotzumalguapa. In the other communities, robbery, assaults, and delinquency were the most commonly ranked as important. Intrafamily violence in particular, and sexual violence in general, also emerged as especially important in a number of communities, often ranked in second or third position (box 2.1).

Perceptions of violence varied by gender and age, and followed broadly similar patterns to those described in relation to problems. For instance, the elderly and adults of both sexes were more reluctant to discuss violence in general. When violence was discussed, elderly and middle-aged women tended to focus on intrafamily and sexual violence, often in relation to alcohol abuse.

Box 2.1   Ranking Types of Violence in Concepción, Guatemala City, Conducted by a Mixed Group of Four Teachers in a Local Primary School

A group of four teachers identified the main types of violence in the community and then voted which they considered the most important. They prioritized both child abuse and child abandonment, reflecting their particular focus on problems affecting the young.

Type of violence	Ranking by votes
Child abuse	3 votes
Child abandonment	3 votes
Gangs	2 votes
Drugs	2 votes
Child sexual abuse	1 vote
Family disintegration	1 vote

Men, on the other hand, concentrated their discussions on robbery, delinquency, and *maras*.

It was among children and adolescents that *maras* were most frequently discussed, with males linking gang members with robbery and delinquency, and females with sexual violence, especially rape. In terms of ethnicity, indigenous groups were more likely to identify political violence in relation to human rights and police abuses than *ladino* groups. However, both indigenous people and *ladinos* equally identified social and economic violence as important problems.

Perceptions of the Spatial Nature of Violence

Within urban areas, many focus groups identified spatial concentrations of violence. These were commonly identified as the *zonas rojas* (red zones) linked with prostitution and drugs, as well as the markets, bus terminals, and sometimes entire communities. In Villa Real, Esquipulas, a group of community leaders noted how the mayor, the municipality, and the rest of the population of the town had until recently labeled the *colonia* as *roja* (red) and *peligrosa* (dangerous). Figure 2.4 shows a map of Santa Lucía Cotzumalguapa, where this group of young men also identified a cemetery and some *colonias* (communities) in addition to these areas.

In addition to the link with drug consumption, there was also a strong association between danger and drunks (the latter sometimes referred to as *bolos*). This was a common pattern in many communities where the *cantinas* (bars) and brothels were usually identified as dangerous. However, women rather than men tended to fear drunks and the *cantinas*; the latter were out of bounds for women of all ages. In addition to places being perceived as dangerous in general, some are only dangerous at night or during the day. Moreover, this may also differ according to gender, with market perceived as more dangerous for women than for men (figure 2.4).

At the community level, maps highlighted concentrations of violence with variations depending on the community. However,

Figure 2.4   Map of dangerous areas of Santa Lucía Cotzumalguapa (drawn by a group of young men aged 20–30)

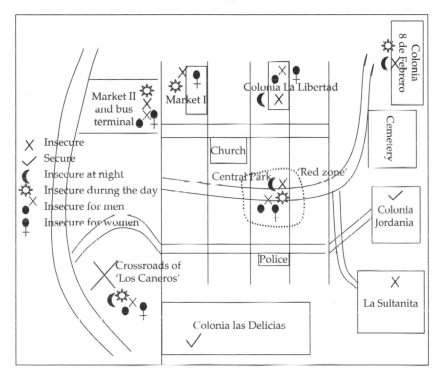

many places identified as dangerous were linked with gangs and, in Guatemala City in particular, with drug consumption. Those most commonly mentioned were football pitches, basketball courts, parks, and riverbanks—all places where gangs congregated. This is particularly marked in the map shown in figure 2.5 of La Merced, Guatemala City. This shows how different gangs are linked with particular spaces and territories within the community, which in turn, are co-opted and become associated with violence and danger.

Figure 2.5   Map of dangerous areas in La Merced, Guatemala City (drawn by a group of young male gang members aged 12–22)

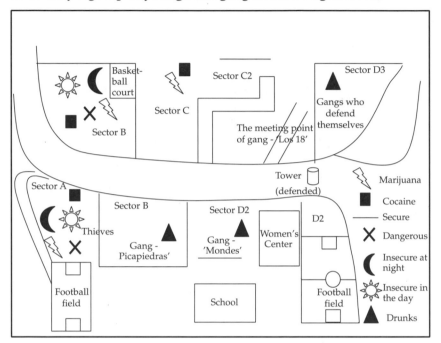

Notes

1. Identification of indigenous people was often difficult, especially in Guatemala City, where many had stopped using traditional dress and used Spanish to communicate (see chapter three).

2. The diagrams do not explicitly refer to ethnic groups because it would have been cumbersome to include this level of detailed information in every focus group discussion.

3. Drugs, for example, are categorized as economic violence, because drug consumers were perceived mainly as a problem linked to robbery to feed their habit. For drug consumers themselves, taking drugs was linked primarily with succumbing to peer pressure, therefore making it a social violence issue.

4. The figures do not add up to 100 percent due to rounding. This applies throughout the text.

3

Political Violence in the Transition to Peace

The legacy of the civil conflict and political violence in Guatemala continues to affect—both directly and indirectly—the nature of conflict in that country today. This legacy provides important contextual background. The particular brutality experienced by the indigenous populations during this period makes it important to comment explicitly on political violence in describing the setting.

Political Violence During the Civil War

In the participatory appraisal, political violence was not viewed as a major issue in the daily lives of the urban poor—an average of only 3 percent of all types of violence identified (table 2.3). Nevertheless, seven of the nine communities identified some political violence, with Gucumatz, Santa Cruz del Quiché; Sacuma, Huehuetenango; and Nuevo Horizonte, Guatemala City, reporting the most. During the civil war political violence was concentrated predominantly in the rural highland region rather than in urban localities. This has shaped present perceptions and patterns of violence in communities in Santa Cruz del Quiché and Huehuetenango. In addition, political violence has left an indelible imprint, especially in Santa Lucía Cotzumalguapa, as well as in some communities in Guatemala City.

Although both *ladino* and indigenous populations were affected by the internal armed conflict, the indigenous population
suffered the most. For instance, the REMHI report (ODHAG 1998)
and the report of the Historical Clarification Commission (CEH
1999) verified the complete destruction of 440 indigenous villages
during the 1980s. Furthermore, the CEH (1999) stated unequivo-
cally that the violence to which the indigenous population was
subjected represented genocide. In the post-conflict context of the
study, political violence was still affecting the indigenous population. For instance, in Gucumatz, Santa Cruz del Quiché, one
indigenous woman commented:

> "Without doubt some political violence is the most
> serious problem that affects Santa Cruz del Quiché.
> It's a problem that is not often verbalized and
> what's more people don't want to discuss it. "

While continuing to affect indigenous populations disproportion-
ately, the legacy of this violence and the resurgence of new forms
of social and economic violence have also affected the *ladino* population, reaching historically unprecedented levels.

Furthermore, some of the counterinsurgency institutions active during the conflict, and now supposedly dissolved, were
identified as a continuing problem in several communities. For
example, the *Patrullas de Autodefensa Civil* (Civil Defense Patrols,
or PACs), although officially disbanded in 1996, were mentioned
in Santa Cruz del Quiché by a group of three *ladino* men who
noted how "the patrols still take people."[1] The same group of
ladinos also mentioned that the army still committed human rights
violations—although less than in the past. Indeed, human rights
violations were mentioned in Guatemala City, Santa Lucía
Cotzumalguapa, and Santa Cruz del Quiché. This counterinsurgency violence and its legacy affected both *ladino* and indigenous ethnic groups. In this context, human rights organizations
continued to be relevant. Previously, human rights organizations
principally represented members of the indigenous population,
but *ladinos* in a Guatemala City community were beginning to

use human rights organizations as a means of resolving intra-family violence.

Despite the decline in political violence as an issue, it influenced and generated other types of violence in Guatemala. Figure 3.1, for instance, shows how armed conflict was associated with a range of different types of political violence, such as massacres, kidnapping, rape, and torture, all linked with delinquency through the migration process (often forced displacement) and lack of employment opportunities.

Changes in Types of Violence in the Post-Conflict Context

Community members reported that, although political violence had declined, other types of economic and social violence were increasing in the post-conflict context. Other than rural communities where widespread massacres took place during the conflict, people reported that they suffered more violence than they had during the worst years of the war. In Santa Cruz del Quiché a group of young indigenous people (aged 14, 15, and 26) discussed changes in violence linked with the *maras*. In 1990, they said there were no *maras* because of the army and guerrilla, but since the Peace Accords some ex-military personnel have joined *maras*. Another group of two men and five women (aged between 25–35, all *ladinos* except one indigenous woman) in Santa Cruz del Quiché discussed the changes in violence. They noted that during the 1980s violence occurred because of the armed conflict, rather than delinquency. Between 1990 and 1995 violence declined, yet after the Peace Accords, delinquency increased—because of the lack of work and because many refugees had returned to Guatemala from Mexico and Honduras. A statement from a group of six women from Sacuma, Huehuetenango, summed up these widespread experiences when they stated "instead of signing peace, they signed violence."

With the end of internal armed conflict, there was a shift from mainly rural-based violence to urban-based violence. Most of the recent increases in violence linked with kidnapping and robberies were perpetrated in the capital region, where a criminal act is reportedly committed every 41 minutes (CIEN 1998:6). There was also a shift toward increasing delinquency in secondary cities and departmental capitals, such as San Marcos and Huehuetenango (Palma 1998). This was a complaint made by community members, especially in the smaller towns.

Political violence that pre-eminently affected the indigenous population during the civil war in the post-conflict context was linked to other forms of economic and social violence. Significantly, this process generated unstable conditions affecting all ethnic groups in both rural and urban areas. A group of three indigenous men (aged between 18 and 33) from Gucumatz, Santa Cruz del Quiché, for instance, said, "Now the same violence affects all of us in the community, *ladinos* and indigenous." A group of three *ladinos*, including two women and one man (aged 15 to 30) from the same community, commented similarly on the changing nature of violence noting, "During the conflict, the indigenous people suffered most from the violence, but now we all have similar experiences of suffering." Comments such as these clearly demonstrate *ladinos'* recognition of the terrible suffering of indigenous people during the conflict, while showing how both groups have been vulnerable to economic and social violence once the Peace Accords were signed.

Other consequences of the internal armed conflict—such as the inefficiency of and lack of confidence in the judicial system, the proliferation of arms, and the breakdown of the social fabric—continued to influence levels of violence in urban communities. This manifested itself in a marked rise in practices of social cleansing and extra-judicial killing, such as lynchings. However, not all consequences were negative. One positive reaction to the inefficiency of the judicial system, linked to the project of indigenous cultural renovation, was the recuperation of indigenous systems of conflict resolution, namely of indigenous customary law. These indigenous alternatives were advocated by social organizations such as Defensoría Maya.

The Culture of Silence

One of the most important legacies of the armed conflict was the culture of silence (*cultura de silencio*). This affected all communities, both indigenous and *ladino*, although it was more widespread in indigenous communities. As a result of human rights violations and the state's counterinsurgency policy during the civil war, silence had been a strategy used by victims of, or witnesses to, violence as a means to avoid violent repercussions. Widespread terror perpetrated during the 1980s, in particular, had created a society based on fear—with its effects on the indigenous population, documented in the REMHI report (ODHAG 1998).[2] As an

Figure 3.1 Causal impact diagram of the effects of armed conflict (prepared by an adult man and an adult woman in La Merced, Guatemala City)

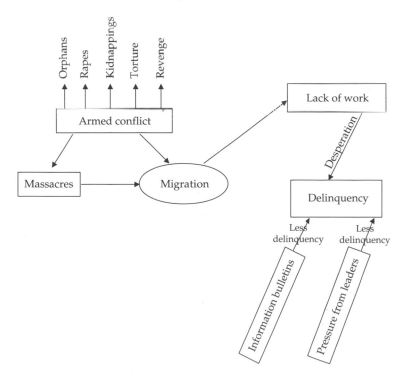

indigenous woman in Santa Cruz del Quiché noted, "Many women do not open their mouths for love of their children."

It is important to emphasize that the culture of silence not only influenced the research findings, but also the research process itself. Because of their fear, people were often reluctant to discuss certain issues. In some cases, they refused to give information or sometimes gave incomplete information. For example, a focus group of four indigenous women working in a tortilla-making shop in Gucumatz, Santa Cruz del Quiché, abruptly ceased talking about an issue when they felt it had become too sensitive. In discussing how violence had changed over time, they said it had been highest in 1978 and then declined in 1982 during the government of Efraín Ríos Montt. They would not carry forward their discussion past 1990, however, choosing instead to simply describe how violence had declined and was now carried out predominantly by thieves. Furthermore, none of the focus groups in Quiché was willing to draw diagrams of the causes and impact of violence. A group of indigenous people from Quiché, comprising a 40-year-old man and two women aged between 40 and 50, simply stated that "people are afraid." Speaking of the conflict, the same group explained how people came from the authorities and asked them their views—if they disagreed with them, they were "taken by the neck." After this happened, people often "changed sides."

Discrimination Against Indigenous People

Racial and cultural discrimination against indigenous people was both a characteristic of the war and part of its continuing legacy. Discrimination did not affect *ladinos* in the research communities, but in all the communities indigenous people referred to it as a problem. For example, in Gucumatz, Santa Cruz del Quiché, one man, describing how discrimination linked political violence in the past and present, said, "Just by being from Quiché, they said that we were guerrilla members, therefore the institutions shut their doors on us." Since the late 1980s indigenous groups began to confront this discrimination to an unprecedented degree, through engagement in a diverse project of ethnic and cultural renovation that precipitated changes in the politico-institutional realm and civil society at local, regional, and national levels. This "Maya Resurgence" (Wilson 1995) challenges historical patterns of discrimination and seeks the institution of a multicultural, multi-ethnic, and pluri-lingual nation-state.[3]

The symbols of indigenous culture were used as a source of discrimination among the *ladino* population in the research communities. An indigenous couple who had fled to La Merced, Guatemala City, during the armed conflict, discussed the declining use of both traditional indigenous dress and language. With respect to the indigenous languages, they noted a marked decline in the use of their mother tongues (he spoke K'iché and she spoke Kachikel) when people came to Guatemala City. While this was partly for practical reasons, it also related to discrimination. For example, a woman explained that often people deliberately did not speak their languages so that others would not know they were indigenous. They said that if they spoke in an indigenous language, then the *ladinos* treated them badly —"they call them Indians."

Another man from San Jorge, Chinautla, for instance, complained that young people were copying *ladino* customs and losing their Pocomam language by mixing Pocomam words with Spanish. Two women in El Carmen, Santa Lucía Cotzumalguapa, originally from Quiché, also cited language as a source of problems. They complained that they didn't like or trust their Spanish-speaking local health center because no one spoke their language. They spoke nostalgically about their *pueblo* (village) and how they could always get an appointment and medicines at the health center in Quiché, unlike in Santa Lucía. The couple from La Merced also expressed sentiments relating to the use of traditional clothing (*traje*). Figure 3.2 illustrates the reasons for not using traditional dress. These included both practical reasons, such as washing difficulties and the lack of economic resources (*traje* is expensive), as well as its association with discrimination.

Another indigenous woman from Nuevo Horizonte, Guatemala City, noted the danger of dressing in *traje* during the war, because of the tendency of the army to identify indigenous people with guerrilla groups. She noted that the army often "pushed

Figure 3.2   Diagram of the reasons for not wearing traditional Mayan dress in La Merced, Guatemala City (drawn by an adult couple)

around" indigenous peoples or kidnapped them when travelling on buses. She said that *ladinos* still referred to them as "dirty" if they wore their traditional clothes of *huipil* (blouse) and *corte* (skirt). As a result, men refused to wear traditional clothes at an even faster rate than women did. In Guatemala City many women would compromise with their traditional clothes and only wear the traditional skirt but not the traditional blouse. Others would wear their indigenous clothes when they returned to their village but change to nontraditional clothes when they went to the city.

Many indigenous groups bemoaned the loss of traditional customs. This was most marked in San Jorge, Chinautla, a predominantly Pocomam community near Guatemala City. A group of three indigenous men—a grandfather and his two grandsons—complained that, because they were close to the capital, young people were copying the customs of the *ladinos* rather than keeping their own cultures. The grandfather noted, "Chinautla feels smaller all the time, like an island surrounded by modernization, and on the road to extinction." A group of five young indigenous women clarified how young people from the capital brought with them bad ideas and habits that were affecting the community.

Poverty and Exclusion

Indigenous focus groups recurrently identified poverty and various types of exclusion as problems, which affirmed the ethnic and gender bias of poverty in Guatemala. Between 80 to 90 percent of the Guatemalan population lived below the U.N.-defined poverty line and up to 75 percent lived in what the U.N. defines as extreme poverty, the latter meaning that they cannot afford even the products that make up the *canasta básica* (or basic food basket) (PNUD 1998; 1999). These figures were more extreme in relation to indigenous groups and women. For example, only 10.5 percent of the indigenous population lived above the poverty line, contrasting to 26 percent for the *ladino* population (PNUD 1998).[4] Poverty was often discussed in association with racial discrimination, especially in terms of access to employment. Indigenous people, with few material resources such as land and education, found it difficult to make ends meet and were most likely to mention poverty as a problem, although some *ladinos* also suffered similar levels of poverty. Discrimination in access to urban employment particularly affected women, who were often forbidden from wearing their traditional clothes and speaking their indigenous languages in the workplace.

Problems in accessing the Guatemala City labor market resulted in many indigenous people migrating to the plantations of Escuintla where seasonal employment required few qualifications or little command of Spanish. A similar process had taken place from the late 1970s onward as indigenous people fled from the political violence in the highland areas of the country. This was especially the case in El Carmen, Santa Lucía Cotzumalguapa. For example, one indigenous couple had fled the violence in Quiché 17 years previously but still complained of a lack of fixed work. The man collected wood for a living, and the woman washed clothes. As a result, they could not afford to send their children to school.

Low levels of educational attainment were also common problems cited by indigenous people. One elderly indigenous woman from El Carmen, Santa Lucía Cotzumalguapa, complained that she thought she was blind because she couldn't read—she had never been to school. The problem, however, as suggested above, was more serious among her children (see figure 3.3 on the causes and effects of illiteracy).

Figure 3.3   Diagram of the causes and effects of illiteracy among the
Mayan population in El Carmen, Santa Lucía Cotzumalguapa
(drawn by a displaced indigenous woman from Quiché)

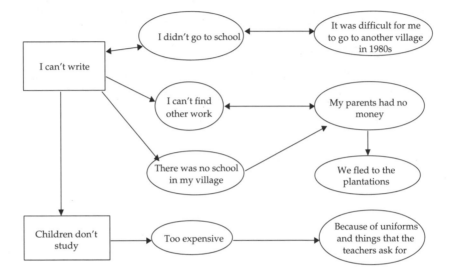

Rape as a Form of Political Violence

The alarming preponderance of rape among all the research communities had important roots in the armed conflict. The REHMI
report documented, for example, how rape was used as a tool of
war and political violence by both the military and the paramili-
tary groups (ODHAG 1999). During the civil war rape became a
fact of life and remained a constant fear for women in the post-
conflict context. While fear of rape was noted by all women, it
was especially so for indigenous women. A group of four indigenous women living in El Carmen, Santa Lucía Cotzumalguapa,
discussed how in 1980 they had fled Nebaj, Quiché, one of the
central arenas of the counterinsurgency, because of "the many
massacres and rapes." They said that as indigenous people they
experienced constant threats from the army, and, as women, this
meant the constant threat of rape—which in this area was primarily perpetrated by the military. One woman described how afraid
she was when living in Nebaj: "We were afraid because the army

came into our homes and killed the people, even though they were innocent." She went on to say, "Many girls and women were raped by the army itself." Yet the same women demonstrated resistance to the tactics of the military, stating, "We wouldn't let the army destroy our people."

Another indigenous woman, who had fled to Guatemala City and lived in La Merced, noted that in general rape was a source of great shame among indigenous people. However, given the scale of rape during the war, parents had to accept daughters who had been raped by the army; often this also included accepting the children who resulted from rape. The same woman noted how raped women rarely married and remained traumatized all their lives.

Political Violence and Household Structure

Armed conflict led to household fragmentation, especially among the indigenous population. In particular, political violence resulted in widespread widowhood, with so many husbands and partners killed. Female household headship, therefore, was very common among indigenous women (see chapter 4).

A group of two indigenous women (aged between 40 and 45) in Gucumatz, Santa Cruz del Quiché, described the predominant types of family structures among indigenous people. Although they described many extended households (comprising grandparents, fathers, mothers, children, uncles, and aunts), they also identified the importance of women-headed households and widows — the consequence of husbands disappearing, or being killed, kidnapped, or assassinated. Box 3.1 highlights the scale of female widowhood. Explaining widowed women's difficulties in making a living in Quiché, the two women noted that their own sources of livelihood were taking in clothes for washing, selling firewood, or making palm plaits for hats, as well as weaving and sewing.

Displaced Populations

During the conflict displaced populations, mainly indigenous, fled as refugees to both Mexico and Honduras. Internal displace-

Box 3.1   Household structure among indigenous people,
in Santa Cruz del Quiché, identified by two indigenous
women aged between 40 and 45 years

Type of household	Number	Reason
Abandoned women	2,000	Because of the emigration linked with lack of work
Widowed women	10,000-15,000	Because of the war; but now there are fewer because some have remarried
Widowed men	1,000	These are those that have not remarried
Women alone	2,000	These are those who have never married
Battered women (sexually and physically)	Majority	Because of the high levels of alcoholism

ment also occurred within Guatemala. During the 1980s indigenous populations moved for political reasons from highland departments to the Ixcán and Sierra regions where the resulting Comunidados de Póblaciones en Resistencia (CPRs)—clandestine mobile communities of indigenous civilians—were targeted by the military, which accused them of being allied to the insurgency. Other indigenous populations moved from Quiché for both political and economic reasons to Guatemala City and Escuintla where they found short-term employment on the plantations.

Displaced people in El Carmen, Santa Lucía Cotzumalguapa, reported how isolated they felt. A 27-year-old indigenous woman said that when she was 14 years old, she and her husband fled Quiché. However, he beat her and had an affair with another woman, so she left him. Her parents and brothers and sisters were killed during the war, and she had no other relatives in El

Carmen, Santa Lucía Cotzumalguapa, except a niece. Another woman now in La Merced, Guatemala City, fled to the capital after seeing her parents killed by the army.

Lynching as a Legacy of the Armed Conflict

Lynchings were also a current major preoccupation in Guatemala. Usually linked with economic violence, lynchings involved a population taking the law into its own hands, usually dousing with petrol and setting alight someone accused of committing a crime, either injuring or killing them.[5] Although lynching did take place in the past, the U.N. mission in Guatemala (MINUGUA) noted that they were taking place at the rate of one per week, mainly in rural areas (1998b:33).[6] While official concern was growing, lynchings were met with public approval. For example, a public opinion survey undertaken in 1996 showed that 75 percent were in favor of taking justice into their own hands (Ferrigno 1998).

The roots of the phenomenon of lynching lay in the armed conflict. Lynchings were concentrated geographically in those areas most affected by the war, such as Huehuetenango and Alta Verapaz. It was suggested that lynchings were most common in departments where the PAC were strongest and most numerous (de León 1998). However, other key causes commonly cited were impunity and lack of confidence in (and effectiveness of) the formal justice system, as well as a history of authoritarianism and the role of the Protestant evangelical church (Ferrigno 1998).

Lynching was part of a wider phenomenon of social cleansing.[7] All the communities identified the presence of lynching, but especially in Santa Cruz del Quiché Huehuetenango; Concepción, Guatemala City; and Santa Lucía Cotzumalguapa. Although many participants reported the experience of lynching, only a few specific cases were identified. In Nuevo Horizonte, Guatemala City, a group of eight young women commented that the lynchings in their community were a good way of dealing with robbery and rape. In La Merced, Guatemala City, participants noted how the recent lynching of a gang of men who had raped a young girl had been precipitated by the inefficiency of the justice system. This was corroborated by the reports of a group of municipal employees (both men and women) from Santa Cruz del Quiché who explained that lynching was integrally related to the impotence of the security forces and legal system.

Political violence in the post-conflict context, as described in this chapter, provided the critical (if often invisible) backdrop for other forms of violence identified through the participatory urban appraisals in the nine research communities. These other forms of violence are discussed in greater depth in the following chapters.

Notes

1. The PAC was created in 1981 in approximately 8,000 communities as a major counterinsurgency tool of the military forces. The PACs were legalized in the 1985 Constitution, by which time it was estimated that 850,000 people (mainly men) belonged, some joining voluntarily, others coerced. The aim of the PAC—with tacit acceptance on the part of the state—was to identify and eliminate dissent and conduct military campaigns in support of the military forces.

2. Koonings and Kruijt (1999:2) point out that: "Of all the countries on the continent, Guatemala is one of the most significant examples of a 'society of fear.'"

3. See Warren (1998) for a detailed discussion.

4. Carol Smith has argued that the ethnic divide reinforces class divisions in Guatemala (1990).

5. MINUGUA notes that 67 percent of those lynched had committed crimes against property. In most cases, they occurred when formal investigations into the offence or crime were not conducted, and people felt moved to punish the accused themselves. In turn, lynchings themselves were rarely investigated (MINUGUA 1998b:33).

6. Between August 1995 and October 1998, 176 lynchings were reported to MINUGUA, making an average of 4.5 per month.

7. Defined as the eradication of particular groups to maintain neighborhood stability; targets are usually criminals, drug-addicts, youth gangs, street children, homosexuals, and prostitutes.

4

Social Violence in the Family and Household

In poor urban Guatemalan communities the local populations prioritized social violence over both political and economic violence. While much of this social violence was endemic both inside people's homes and outside in the streets and bars, the particular anxieties, fears, and tensions inherent in the post-conflict context have also taken their toll on human relationships, among *ladino* and indigenous populations alike. This chapter focuses on social violence within the family. Chapters 5 and 6 then examine social violence outside the home in terms of its close association with alcohol, drugs, and bar and street fights.

Household Structure

Intrafamily violence requires contextualization in terms of the predominant structures of households in the study communities (see chapter 2). Information from focus group discussions on community characteristics showed clearly the diversity of household structures that existed. A number of issues emerged as important. First, reportedly less than half of all households were nuclear (male-headed, two-parent with children), representing an average of 46 percent of all households across communities. These ranged from a low of one-third of all households in San Jorge, Chinautla, to 59 percent in Limoncito, San Marcos.

Also significant was the high proportion of households headed by single female parents, known as "single mothers," particularly among indigenous women (see chapter 3). A group of three women in La Merced, Guatemala City, for instance, estimated that single women headed 40 percent of all households in the community. Indeed, they specifically noted that there were five single mothers in every block within the community. Proportions were also high in Gucumatz, Santa Cruz del Quiché; one group of two indigenous women and one man estimated that 60 percent of households were headed by females, while another group of seven middle-aged indigenous women suggested that the figure was nearer 30 percent.

The causes of female headship were seen as diverse. In some cases, especially in Santa Cruz del Quiché and some Guatemala City communities, they were linked with the civil war. This was reflected in the high proportion of indigenous widows among single mothers, as well as women who had been raped by military men and became pregnant as a result. Also important was migration to the United States that left many women as de facto female heads; this was especially common in Santa Cruz del Quiché and Villa Real, Esquipulas. In the latter, for example, one focus group estimated that 70 percent of families in the community had relatives living in the United States. Abandonment of wives by husbands and vice versa was also linked with *machismo*, alcohol abuse, and intrafamily violence (see below).

In addition to nuclear and female-headed, single-parent households, other common types of households were headed by grandparents, representing an average of around 12 percent of all households. In some cases again this was linked to the civil war, where children were left orphaned, as well as abandoned when parents migrated to the United States. Another interesting phenomenon was the number of households headed by single fathers living alone with their children. In total this was around 5 percent; yet according to one focus group this figure was as high as 30 percent of all households in La Merced, Guatemala City. Finally, there were also many male- and female-headed extended households. In some cases, these referred to single-parent subfamilies or embedded female heads (where single mothers were absorbed into large extended households). However, many focus groups noted how extended households often comprised a range of aunts, uncles, cousins, nephews, and nieces. These were especially common in the Guatemala City communities due to relatives migrating from the provinces to the city to find work in the capital.

The Nature and Scope of Intrahousehold or Intrafamily Violence[1]

Intrafamily violence emerged as a major preoccupation in listings of types of problems and in listings of types of violence in the nine communities. In the listings of problems, for instance, intrafamily violence was the third most important type of violence-related problem mentioned (annex B, table B.1). In the violence listings, social violence was the highest single category of violence affecting the communities, with violence inside the home representing 14 percent of all types of violence cited, and fights outside the home representing 28 percent (table 2.3). There were important variations among the nine communities. The highest level was identified in San Jorge, Chinautla (29 percent), and the lowest in Sacuma, Huehuetenango (6 percent). No obvious reasons for such variations emerged, although Chinautla had one of the highest proportions of indigenous populations. However, in Gucumatz, Santa Cruz del Quiché, which also has a high proportion of indigenous population, the figure was far lower (11 percent).

It is also significant that other types of social violence outside the home were twice as common as intrafamily violence (28 percent and 14 percent, respectively) (table 2.3). This may relate to the culture of silence; people were afraid to talk about violence for fear of retribution from others. Although this affected all of the violence discussions (see chapter 3), it was particularly pertinent to intrafamily violence. The taboo meant that often it was only possible to explore intrafamily violence from the perspective of alcohol abuse. Since alcohol was often identified as the cause of domestic male–female violence, this provided an entry point in focus groups for discussions of the issue.

In contrast, children and younger people were often more candid about the issue of intrafamily violence. Nevertheless the language used was general and nonspecific, as illustrated in the 18 different types of intrafamily violence identified from all communities (box 4.1). Types of violence included verbal, physical, and sexual abuse. Probably the most disarming fact that emerged was that the family as a unit itself was perceived as violent, and within it all social actors were involved in violence, as either perpetrators or victims. The relationships among three different sets of social actors within families emerged as most important in terms of intrafamily violence: spouses, children, and youth.

Violence Between Spouses

Violence between spouses was so widespread that it was an assumed occurrence within households. In the vast majority of

---

Box 4.1   Composite listing of types of intrafamily violence

- Verbal abuse and quarrels
- Physical fighting
- Men verbally abusive to spouses
- Men physically beat/hit their wives
- Sexual violence against wives
- Parents hit their children (to correct them)
- Fathers hit their sons
- Mothers hit their sons
- Sexual abuse of children
- Robbery of children
- Rape of girls and young women
- Rape and strangulation of young women
- Brothers beat each other
- Sexual abuse between brothers
- Killing between brothers
- Young men hit their fathers
- Older children hit younger ones
- Violence against the elderly

Source: 154 violence listings and 199 problem listings.

cases, men were the perpetrators and women the victims. However, one focus group in La Merced, Guatemala City, noted that in 5 percent of cases of inter-spousal violence women were perpetrators. The most common type was physical abuse—wife beating—that men usually inflicted when drunk (chapter 5). This usually involved men hitting their wives with their fists but sometimes included knives and machetes. Numerous women who had escaped their husbands' violence said that they feared for their lives, as mentioned by a 35-year-old market seller from Limoncito, San Marcos. She left her drunken husband, not only because he constantly beat her, but also because he threatened to kill her with knives.

Women rarely mentioned sexual violence on the part of husbands, mainly because of the expectation that they would serve their partners sexually. However, many women discussed verbal and psychological violence. There were numerous examples of women being told they were worthless by husbands. In La Merced, a single mother who left her husband said that he came home every night and told her she was "useless." She added that many women suffered from low self-esteem and psychological trauma because they believed the accusations made by their husbands.

Violence Against Children

Violence against children was also alarmingly widespread, and was referred to as "child abuse" (*maltrato infantil*) by community members. A group of five young girls (aged between 9 and 14) in Gucumatz, Santa Cruz del Quiché, noted that 85 percent of children suffered violence in the home. Violence against children took a number of forms and involved both mothers and fathers as perpetrators. For instance, a particularly common form was the physical beating of disobedient sons and daughters. Although not all parents necessarily considered this a form of violence, the participatory urban appraisal as a methodology also reflected the voices of children and adolescents. These groups were strongly opposed to this form of physical attack by parents.

Sexual abuse was the main other type of violence experienced by children, with fathers, the main perpetrators, abusing their daughters. In Concepción, Guatemala City, for instance, a group of five primary-school students described how a father raped his daughter, who lived nearby. Since the father also beat her mother, the daughter felt she couldn't tell her mother for fear that the father would kill her. Another group of four teachers from the same community commented, "Often the mothers don't believe what their children are saying, because they're afraid of losing their husbands." In another example from Gucumatz, Santa Cruz del Quiché, in a focus group of seven, each woman cited an example of an incest case with which they were all familiar.

Sexual violence or incest perpetrated by stepfathers was the most serious form of intrafamily violence. In one example a man simultaneously fathered three children: one by his wife, and two more by two stepdaughters whom he had abused. In El Carmen, Santa Lucía Cotzumalguapa, a group of three women discussed how stepfathers raped their stepdaughters when the mothers were out at work. Stepfathers were also seen as responsible for physical as well as sexual abuse. The focus group in Santa Cruz del Quiché recounted the experience of a young girl who returned from a party to her waiting stepfather. During an ensuing argument caused by his jealousy, he cut off her hair with scissors and then stabbed her in the head.

Uncles within extended households were also identified as perpetrators who often took advantage of girls. Although it was mainly girls who suffered, in a minority of cases boys also suffered sexual violence. Teachers, in particular, noted the impact of incest on children's behavior in school.[2] Figure 4.1, drawn by a 13-year-old girl, illustrated the fear of being sexually abused while asleep.

Violence Among Children and Youth

In addition to intergenerational violence, widespread physical and verbal fights within the home among siblings were also common. In San Jorge, Chinautla, for example, a group of three girls (aged 14 to 15) discussed how they argued with their siblings over household tasks. While most of the conflict was verbal, it sometimes erupted into violence, especially on the part of brothers. Sexual violence among children in the home was also men-

Figure 4.1   Drawing of sexual violence against children in the home (drawn by a 13-year-old girl from El Carmen, Santa Lucía Cotzumalguapa)

Note: Translation of text: "I'm afraid that when I'm sleeping I could be raped, that's what I'm afraid of."

tioned. In La Merced, Guatemala City, two women (aged 25 and 35) mentioned that sexual relations sometimes occurred between siblings, when children were left at home on their own while their mothers were at work.

Factors Affecting the Level of Intrafamily Violence

Intrafamily violence in communities was viewed as deep-seated, stretching back centuries. As one woman from Gucumatz, Santa Cruz del Quiché, noted, "Violence in the home has always existed."

Alcohol abuse was identified as the primary cause of intrafamily violence (chapter 5 provides a more detailed description of the phenomenon). In all discussions of intrafamily violence, and especially violence against women and children, alcoholism was mentioned (figure 4.2). Women repeatedly complained that when men came home from the *cantina* they beat their wives and children. In La Merced, Guatemala City, one woman reported how she hated the smell of alcohol, since it always reminded her of being beaten by her husband. She said that when she smelt it on her husband's breath she jumped out of bed and fled the house so he couldn't beat her.

Infidelity was cited as another major cause, again mainly linked with wife abuse. Although this included infidelity by both women and men (figure 4.2), it referred mainly to male unfaithfulness. A focus group of four women from La Merced, Guatemala City, cited "third parties" as one of the main causes of intraspouse conflict. They said that on average women gave husbands three chances to be unfaithful, after which the relationship was over. Infidelity was also linked with jealousy. Violent arguments often erupted as a result of accusations between men and women.

Underlying violence against women and children was the so-called phenomenon of *machismo*—men (referred to as

Figure 4.2 Causal impact diagram of mistreatment of women in El Carmen, Santa Lucía Cotzumalguapa (drawn by a mixed sex group of four students and one young woman aged 18–22))

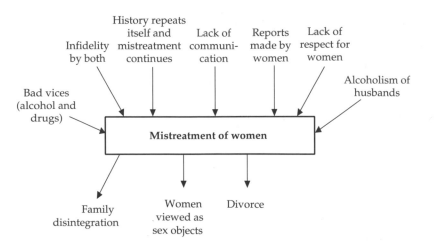

machistas) using physical force as an expression of power over women. This was also linked with lack of respect for women (figure 4.2). Although *machistas* were not necessarily violent, most men who perpetrated violence in the home were *machistas*. Also linked with *machismo* was the fact that women often blamed themselves for being beaten by men. A group of four women in El Carmen, Santa Lucía Cotzumalguapa, said that they expected to be abused if they didn't look after their husbands properly in terms of cooking, cleaning, and washing clothes. Among the few men who discussed gender-based violence, an important motive for beating women was identified as their failure to perform their household duties.

Consequences of Intrafamily Violence

Family Disintegration and the Erosion of Social Capital Endowments

When focus groups preferred not to discuss violence openly, they used the term "family disintegration" as a euphemism for intrafamily violence, which was identified as a major cause and consequence of familial conflict. Intrafamily violence undermined the way households functioned internally in terms of constructing norms, values, and trust (social capital). Since family relations provided a primary source of cognitive social capital, the outcome of the interrelated processes of intrafamily violence and family disintegration was the severe undermining of cognitive social capital endowments.

Many of the causes of family disintegration were similar to those associated more generally with intrafamily violence. These included infidelity and *machismo* (figure 4.3). However, intrafamily violence itself was also a cause of family disintegration (figure 4.3). Other factors mentioned included "lack of understanding" and "lack of affection" between parents and children. A group of three young girls (aged 13 and 14) from Concepción, Guatemala City, complained that a lack of parental support was a major issue affecting their lives. One of them complained, "I feel sad, sometimes they don't even love us." Another

Figure 4.3   Causal impact diagram of family disintegration in Limoncito, San Marcos (prepared by a mixed group of six primary school teachers)

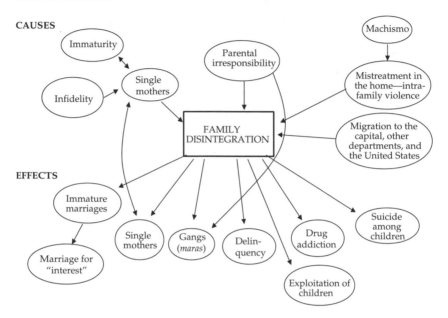

went as far as to say that other relatives understood them better than their own parents—who were often fighting anyway. The third girl pointed out that they sometimes had to miss a year's schooling as a result of their parents' failure to understand its importance.

A mixed group of young people (all aged 17) from El Carmen, Santa Lucía Cotzumalguapa, identified who benefited and who lost out in cases of family disintegration. They said that men benefited because they got another woman and that the beer-producing company, *Gallo*, increased its profits because men drank more beer. In addition, they suggested that *maras* benefited because children's parents no longer went out to look for them, and prostitutes were better off because they made more money. Children, wives, and society all lost out: children because they were left alone, wives because they were left with no money and more responsibility, and society because women and children were ignored.

Intrafamily Violence Creates Single-Mother Households

Another consequence of intrafamily violence was a change in household structure. This was associated with the creation of single-parent households, especially those headed by women (figure 4.3). Many single parents identified discrimination against them as a major problem, while others cited single motherhood as an important societal problem in itself. Some community members noted that abusive partners often abandoned their wives to live with other women with whom they had been having an affair. A group of adult women from El Carmen, Santa Lucía Cotzumalguapa, felt that single motherhood was caused by men getting tired of their wives, beating them, and finding younger women who had more money. In addition, women often married too young without getting to know beforehand whether or not husbands were violent.

Equally, women were increasingly leaving abusive men. A group of single mothers from La Merced, Guatemala City, noted that many women who could no longer cope with the violence and *machismo* of their husbands left them. Although they said that leaving their husband was a last resort, it was often the only option when women feared for their lives (figure 4.4).

Intrafamily Violence Leads to Violence Outside the Home

Intrafamily violence generated other types of violence, including gang activity, drug addiction, and delinquency. Focus groups identified a process that started with intrafamily violence that led first to family disintegration and then to children and youth involvement in street violence. Children who had suffered or witnessed violence in the home were more likely to escape family problems by turning to the streets. This often involved gang activity where the *maras* provided a form of social support lacking in the family (see chapter 7). Sometimes this was linked to substance abuse, usually in the form of drugs among young people (see chapter 6). A group of teachers from El Carmen, Santa Lucía Cotzumalguapa, made a direct link between family disintegration and drug addiction. They said that when children felt

Figure 4.4 Causal flow diagram of the causes of single motherhood in La Merced, Guatemala City (drawn by a group of four adult women aged between 18 and 48)

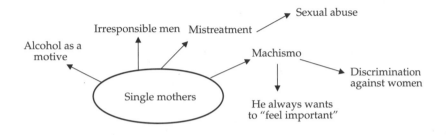

"unloved" and were subject to abuse in the home, they often turned to drugs for solace.

Three women from Nuevo Horizonte, Guatemala City, distinguished between two potential outcomes of intrafamily violence for young people (figure 4.5). They identified one route

Figure 4.5 Causal impact diagram of intrafamily violence in Nuevo Horizonte, Guatemala City (prepared by three women aged 39, 20, and 18)

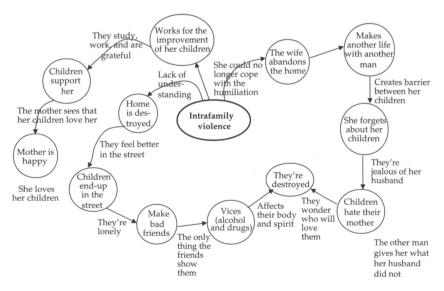

where the wife and mother remained loyal to her children; in the other she found another partner, creating other problems for the children, who could get involved with bad company and turn to drugs and alcohol.

Intergenerational Conflict and the Erosion of Human Capital

Conflict between parents and children was both a cause and consequence of intrafamily violence. Teachers in particular noted that the lack of discipline in the home often led to violence and disintegration. A mixed group of teachers from Limoncito, San Marcos, for instance, blamed the low educational levels of the parents, and what they called "lack of culture," for intergenerational problems. They linked the causes of conflict to *machismo* and infidelity (figure 4.6), highlighting the severe effects. Male children became "good-for-nothings," alcoholics, drug addicts, or joined *maras*, while female children became single mothers or prostitutes.

Figure 4.6 Causal flow diagram of intergenerational conflict between parents and children in Limoncito, San Marcos (prepared by a mixed group of six teachers)

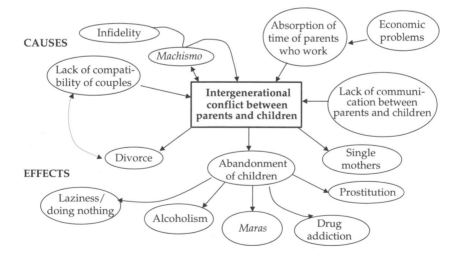

People rarely intervened or helped victims of intrafamily violence or abuse. Three women in Nuevo Horizonte, Guatemala
City, for instance, stated that despite the widespread phenomenon of child abuse, people were afraid to intervene for fear of
reprisals from neighbors. Similar responses to wife beating were
discussed. A focus group of three women from La Merced, Guatemala City, said that they only called the police when a husband
was seriously harming his wife; otherwise they kept quiet. In the
post-conflict context of Guatemala few people trusted anyone,
and people still lived in constant fear of speaking out against
others. The lack of cognitive social capital that pervaded the study
communities is further explored in chapter 8.

Notes

1. The terms "family" and "household" are used interchangeably. However, it is also recognized that the latter refers more specifically to the resi-
dential unit, while the latter is more broadly conceived and may include
relatives not living within a particular household unit. The term "family"
also incorporates more intangible notions such as value systems. The same
applies to the distinction between intrafamily and intrahousehold violence.
However, more frequently it is referred to as intrafamily violence, as this is
the term used by people in the communities themselves.

2. Children also complained of teachers beating them in school; in some
extreme cases this caused children to withdraw altogether from school.

5

Social Violence
and Alcohol Consumption

S ocial violence outside the home was primarily linked with alcohol. Heavy alcohol consumption was a major problem in all nine communities both as a problem in itself, and in terms of its links to other types of violence. Outside the home, it was closely related with street fighting and disturbances in local *cantinas*, while inside the home, it was linked with intrafamily violence, especially against women and children.

Alcohol- and drug-related violence was associated with 23 percent of all violence-related problems in the study communities (see tables 5.1 and 6.1), with alcohol-related violence representing an average of 10 percent of all violence-related problems. Variations reveal that alcohol-related violence was reported as most common in Limoncito, San Marcos, and in El Carmen, Santa Lucía Cotzumalguapa (table 5.1).

Because they were viewed as endemic, or "normal," alcohol-related problems tended to be underreported. With such a long history of alcohol abuse in the communities, it was frequently not mentioned as a problem. In all communities the phrase "there has always been alcoholism here" was repeated, signifying that heavy drinking was viewed as a normal activity. This accounted for the differences in reported figures for alcoholism as compared to drug-related problems.

Table 5.1   Alcohol-related violence as proportion of all violence-related problems *(percentage)*

Community	Violence-related problem as a percent of all problems	Alcohol-related violence as a percent of all violence-related problems
Concepción, Guatemala City	54	7
Nuevo Horizonte, Guatemala City	51	12
La Merced, Guatemala City	46	11
San Jorge, Chinautla	33	12
Sacuma, Huehuetenango	60	7
Limoncito, San Marcos	49	16
El Carmen, Santa Lucía Cotzumalguapa	47	15
Villa Real, Esquipulas	36	8
Gucumatz, Santa Cruz del Quiché	51	14
Total	**48**	**10**

Source: 199 focus group listings of general problems.

Types of Alcohol-Related Problems

While alcohol in itself is not a type of violence, it is closely associated with violent behavior and conflict within communities. Alcohol-related violence was categorized as social violence, mainly because it involved the use of violence for the exercise of social power, although in some cases in the study it involved economic violence—when inebriated people stole money to buy alcohol. In El Carmen, Santa Lucía Cotzumalguapa, for instance, one focus group noted how men from the local *cantinas* would rob people coming from the market in order to get enough money to buy more rum. For this reason, people avoided walking near the bars.

Overall, people in the communities identified 16 different types of problems related to alcohol (box 5.1). Most commonly they cited "alcoholism"—a catchall term for a range of problems and conflicts. These included problems ranging from street fights

---

Box 5.1   Alcohol-related problems identified in nine communities

Alcoholism
Clandestine alcohol consumption
Drunks lying around in the streets
Drunken youth
Fights among drunk men in the streets
Bar (*cantina*) fights
Knife attacks by drunks
Drunk men fire guns in the air in the street
Men urinate outside bars and contaminate the community
Men expose themselves to young girls when they urinate in
    the street
Alcoholic women
Alcohol-induced rape of women
Drunks killed in traffic accidents
Drunks frighten children in the street
Drunks hassle people for money in the street
Children grow up traumatized because of alcoholism

Source: 199 listings of problems and 154 listings of violence.

---

among drunks, to drunken men raping women and girls, inside and outside the home. Indeed, the link between alcohol abuse and sexual violence in the streets and in the home was particularly strong in all the communities. Also common was street fighting associated with alcohol abuse. These were generally fistfights, although occasionally they involved gun fights (especially in Villa Real, Esquipulas). In the majority of cases it was men who fought, although arguments were often over women.

Changes in Alcohol Consumption over Time

Heavy alcohol consumption has been widespread in most communities for as long as people can remember, reflected in the fact that all communities had an Alcoholics Anonymous group located within the *colonia* (see chapter 8). Despite heavy overall consumption, people noted variations across shorter time frames. Over the period of a year, for instance, peak times identified for alcohol consumption and alcohol-related violence were New Year, Easter, Mother's Day, Independence Day, and Christmas (figure 5.1). Celebratory occasions such as these were closely associated with large consumption of alcohol. Many focus groups noted increasing or decreasing levels of intrafamily violence relating directly to alcohol consumption levels over different time periods. For example, a group of four women from La Merced, Guatemala City, directly linked the week days when men were more likely to drink—Friday, Saturday, and Sunday, and sometimes Monday—to the days when most intrafamily violence occurred. Men were paid on Friday or Saturday and then drank until the following Monday.[1] In all communities, the most important drinking day was Sunday. In addition to increased intrafamily violence over the weekend, the number of robbery and assaults grew when it was known that paid workers had money in their pockets and were less vigilant under the influence of alcohol.

Figure 5.1 Timeline showing changes in alcohol consumption and related violence over the period of one year (prepared by an 83-year-old man in San Jorge, Chinautla

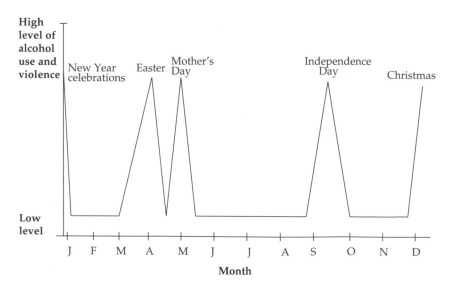

Linked with this cycle, fights in the bars and the streets also rose over weekends.

Types of Alcohol Available

In the research communities a number of different types of alcohol were common. While beer was most widespread, it was rarely linked with heavy drinkers or alcoholics, who usually drank various types of rum or, if desperate, antiseptic alcohol (box 5.2). In La Merced, Guatemala City, a woman street stall–owner selling beer noted the distinction between alcoholics who consumed *guaro* (rum) or chemicals, and social drinkers who drank beer. Illegal or clandestine alcohol made from fermented fruit—known variously as *kuto*, *kuxa*, and *kusha*—was also mentioned in three communities.

In Santa Cruz del Quiché and Esquipulas clandestine alcohol was freely available in the local *cantinas*. In the former, for instance, a police official reported that this was an extremely cheap, traditional drink, especially among the Maya population. A focus group of 14 adults from the same community ranked clandestine alcohol as the most important problem affecting them. They blamed its pervasive use on poverty—since it was the cheapest available.[2] They maintained that the authorities (the police) did nothing to curb its sale, in some cases even buying it themselves. The group listed a range of consequences, including vio-

---

Box 5.2   Types of alcohol available

Beer
Guaro (rum)
Aguardiente (rum)
Antiseptic alcohol
Químicos (chemicals—methylated spirits)
Kuto (clandestine alcohol)
Kusha (clandestine alcohol)
Kuxa (clandestine alcohol)

Source: Focus groups in nine communities.

lence against women and children, rape, incest, and family disintegration, as well as further impoverishment.

Characteristics of Alcohol Consumers

Alcoholics and heavy drinkers were called a range of names in addition to *alcohólicos* (alcoholics): *borachos*, *bolos*, *charamileros*, or *charamilos* (when someone is physically disintegrating because of alcohol abuse), and *chibolas*. As well as using the verb "to drink," other verbs such as *chupar* ("to suck") were used.

While some indigenous groups reported especially high levels of alcohol use linked with trauma and poverty, alcohol abuse was widespread regardless of ethnic group. The majority of heavy drinkers in communities were male. In El Carmen, Santa Lucía Cotzumalguapa, for example, three women (aged in their twenties) noted that 90 percent of men in the community drank heavily and dangerously. Similarly, in La Merced, Guatemala City, a woman, whose husband had been killed in a traffic accident when drunk, maintained that 75 percent of men were alcoholics. Usually the only men who did not drink heavily were those who belonged to one of the evangelical churches that required a vow of abstinence.

However, some women also drank heavily. For instance, a 40-year-old man in La Merced, Guatemala City, suggested that for every 100 adult women, 60 drank alcohol. However, he also pointed out that few women had drinking problems, whereas most men were heavy drinkers. Similarly, a focus group of adult women in Villa Real, Esquipulas, said that 50 percent of all men were alcoholics, whereas 25 percent of all women drank heavily. While men drank in public, usually in the *cantinas*, women drank at home in private. In contrast, a 52-year-old woman in Sacuma, Huehuetenango, noted that women also drank in *cantinas*, with women often found unconscious on the pavements alongside drunken men. Also important is that it was drunken men rather than inebriated women who were associated with violence. All age groups drank alcohol, with many boys starting at 12, 13, or 14 years of age (according to a 17-year-old woman in Santa Cruz del Quiché). When compared with drug use, alcohol was associated with the more mature, while drugs were linked with youth (see chapter 6).

Causes of Heavy Alcohol Consumption

Many communities listed the same key causes of heavy alcohol consumption. Most common was the notion that poverty caused a level of desperation that made some men drink heavily. This was closely linked to unemployment. In Sacuma, Huehuetenango, for instance, two women in their thirties noted that because there was no work there were lots of drunks in the streets. They observed that in the past the government had cleared the streets of drunks and sent them off to public works schemes. Similarly, in Gucumatz, Santa Cruz del Quiché, three men (aged between 14 and 26 years) cited poverty and disillusionment as the key causes of alcoholism. Figure 5.2 highlights poverty and disillusionment as primary causes, according to a focus group from La Merced, Guatemala City.

Figure 5.2   Causal impact diagram of men who drink in La Merced, Guatemala City (drawn by three women aged 16, 34, and 40 years)

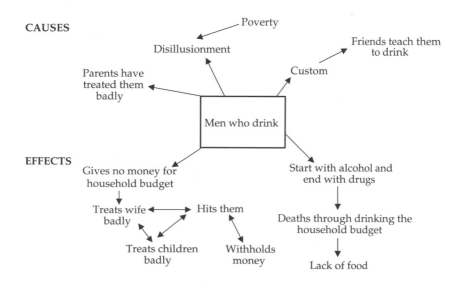

Family problems were also frequently cited as root causes of alcoholism. In figures 5.2 and 5.3, for instance, parental mistreatment was identified as a key reason for turning to alcohol abuse. A 40-year-old woman from Nuevo Horizonte, Guatemala City, stated that when parents drank in front of their children, the children were likely to learn to drink. Heavy drinking usually resulted from intrafamily violence, especially when fathers, under the influence of alcohol, beat their children. Both marital conflict and disappointment in a romantic affair were identified as causes inducing men to drink heavily. The focus group from Nuevo Horizonte, Guatemala City and Villa Real, Esquipulas, for example, distinguished such causal factors as "because your wife treats you badly" and "marriage without love, or premature marriage" (figures 5.3 and 5.4).

Other causal factors were associated with "bad company" and peer pressure (figures 5.2 and 5.3). Drinking alcohol was a major leisure pursuit in most communities, revolving primarily around *cantinas*, and, to a lesser extent, brothels. Men went directly to the *cantinas* after work and often spent all their free time drink-

Figure 5.3   Causal relations diagram of alcoholism in Nuevo Horizonte, Guatemala City (prepared by five adult women and one man)

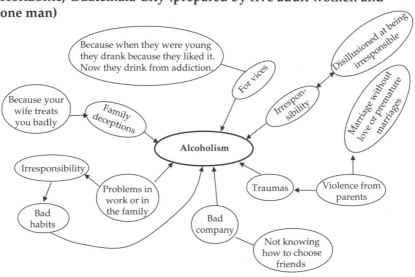

Figure 5.4 Problem tree of alcoholism in Villa Real, Esquipulas (drawn by two women aged 35 and 17 and one man aged 15)

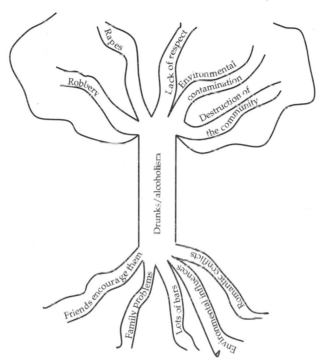

ing with friends. One woman in Limoncito, San Marcos, complained that her husband was a heavy drinker who forgot about his wife and children when he drank with his friends. Indeed, she blamed his friends for turning him into an alcoholic.

Consequences of Heavy Alcohol Consumption

The consequences of heavy alcohol consumption were both economic and social, and related to different types of violence. Economic hardship within households, caused by breadwinners using the family budget to buy alcohol, was most commonly cited. Women, in particular, noted how they were often left without food to feed their children, because their husbands had drunk the family budget. In figure 5.2 a focus group shows that alcohol and drug abuse can lead to the death of family members, which through the subsequent lack of labor capacity in the household can lead to the family having less food. In another case from San Jorge, Chinautla, a middle-aged man noted that, "Rum kills everything; many sell all they own in order to be able to drink." Another woman from Villa Real, Esquipulas, stated that alcohol destroys the home; not only does it mean that the family is left with no food, but alcoholics lose their jobs as well.

Alcoholism was also associated with indebtedness within communities. Two carpenters in Villa Real, Esquipulas, noted that very few carpenters did not drink heavily, and, as a result, all of them owed money. They often developed debt relief networks among themselves since they regularly spent 100 percent of their weekly earnings. If not spending on their own alcohol consumption, they bought drinks for their friends. One carpenter noted that many women had to go out to work because their husbands drank all their wages.

One of the main violence-related consequences of heavy drinking was an increase in intrafamily violence.[3] Although conjugal conflict was perceived as a cause of alcoholism, it was more commonly seen as an outcome. This was not only associated with verbal, physical, and sexual violence against women, but also with the mistreatment of children. In some extreme cases alcoholism was blamed for husbands killing their wives. In Villa Real, Esquipulas, for example, a number of focus groups noted that there had been cases of men killing their wives when they were drunk. In another case, a young boy of 10 from La Merced, Guatemala City, noted that because his father was a drunk he hid from him when he came home from the *cantina*. He also pointed out that his father often sent him out to buy rum or marijuana from local shops or dealers.

Alcohol, both legal and clandestine, was also associated with sexual violence in the streets, particularly the rape of women and girls. In Concepción, Guatemala City, five mothers identified the community's main problem as rapes of local girls by drunks. In a number of communities, drunk men also urinated in the streets and exposed themselves, which are referred to as "environmental contamination and lack of respect" in figure 5.4 from Villa

Real, Esquipulas. In Gucumatz, Santa Cruz del Quiché, women and children were afraid to go near bars, because of the threat of rape; in El Carmen, Santa Lucía Cotzumalguapa, an 11-year-old girl said that she didn't like going near the *cantina* because of the drunks who "touched her."

Also related with *cantinas* were fights among men. In all communities, people reported brawls among men who had drunk too much. In Villa Real, Esquipulas, in particular, street fighting linked with alcohol was especially widespread. Here, drunk men went around the community shooting their guns indiscriminately. Another related problem was "crimes of passion," which involved assassinations during bar or brothel fights. For example, one woman who owned a shop in the community reported how her husband had been shot the previous year in the local brothel during a drunken fight over a prostitute.

Alcohol consumption is an important problem in the research communities. It is also increasingly perceived to be interrelated with drug consumption as a cause of violence, as discussed in the next chapter.

Notes

1. Monday was referred to as *día de caldo* or *caldo de mano*, which translates roughly as the "day of the bull." On this day local *cantinas* prepared a stew from bull meat or shellfish reputedly as a hangover cure. However, often men who went to the *cantina* for the *caldo* ended up drinking heavily again.

2. In Villa Real, Esquipulas, a bottle of *kuto* cost 2 *quetzales*, whereas a liter of beer cost 10 *quetzales* and a quarter bottle of rum cost 3.75 *quetzales* (at the time of the study $1=7 *Quetzales*).

3. In a number of cases the only way women would talk about intrafamily violence was through discussing alcohol abuse in communities. From a methodological perspective, this provided the means for introducing this sensitive issue into focus group discussions.

6

Economic Violence
and Drug Consumption

In urban communities drug-related problems were perceived as more serious than those relating to alcohol, despite the fact that the actual consequences of drug-related violence were less acute than those resulting from alcohol. This difference in perception was influenced by the fact that while alcohol-related problems were endemic in communities, those relating to drugs were far newer and consequently were considered to be more alarming.

Drug-related problems were a major concern in communities, linked to 13 percent of all violence-related problems (table 6.1), yet the importance of drug-related problems varied across communities. In Nuevo Horizonte, for example, drugs were identified as related to 20 percent of all violence-related problems. In contrast, in El Carmen, Santa Lucía Cotzumalguapa, drugs were perceived to be related to only 6 percent (table 6.1).

Types of Drug-Related Problems

The difference in perceptions about drug-related versus alcohol-related problems was due to the fact that drugs were a relatively new phenomenon, whereas alcohol abuse had become a way of life. Of the different drug-related problems cited, drug addiction

Table 6.1   Drug-related violence as a proportion of all violence-related problems

Community	Violence-related problems as a percent of all problems	Drug related violence as a percent of all violence-related problems
Concepción, Guatemala City	54	7
Nuevo Horizonte, Guatemala City	51	20
La Merced, Guatemala City	46	13
San Jorge, Chinautla	33	9
Sacuma, Huehuetenango	60	13
Limoncito, San Marcos	49	12
El Carmen, Santa Lucía Cotzumalguapa	47	6
Villa Real, Esquipulas	36	17
Gucumatz, Santa Cruz del Quiché	51	12
Total	**48**	**13**

Source: 199 focus group listings of general problems.

was most commonly identified as a general problem affecting communities (box 6.1).

Overall, 10 different drug-related problems were identified. While drug-taking itself was not necessarily violent, drug consumption was a crime. In addition, drug-taking was often associated with economic violence, because of the petty theft and robbery undertaken for cash needed to feed drug habits. This tended to be more widespread than robbery linked with alcohol abuse. Other violence associated with drug consumption included sexual violence (such as rape) and delinquency (such as throwing stones and fighting among gangs). Violence linked to drug distribution was also mentioned frequently, especially in relation to *narcotraficantes* (drug dealers).

In terms of variations among the communities, drug-related problems were perceived as much more serious in *colonias* in Guatemala City and in the border towns of Huehuetenango and

---

Box 6.1   Types of drug-related problems identified in nine communities

Drug addiction
Drug distribution
Drug consumption
Gang fights over drugs
Social cleansing of drug addicts
Glue sniffing
Robbery by drug addicts
Rapes by drug addicts
Drug-addicted delinquents
Youth drug violence

Source: 199 listings of problems and 154 listings of violence.

Esquipulas than in other communities. In communities with greater access to different drugs, people tended to be more knowledgeable about both drug consumption and distribution.

Changes in Drug Consumption over Time

While drug consumption was a relatively new phenomenon in all the communities, it became a serious issue in the 1990s and, in many cases, had increased since the signing of the Peace Accords in 1996. Drug consumption tended to have a longer history in Guatemala City than in other places. In Concepción, Guatemala City, for example, a group of three adult women and two female adolescents said that drug consumption had been increasing steadily since 1989. In contrast, in El Carmen, Santa Lucía Cotzumalguapa, drug trafficking and consumption had become problems more recently (1998–99). A group of six men noted that the *narcos* (drug dealers) had emerged as a new phenomenon in 1999; these traffickers paid local farmers or farm administrators to use their cane fields as landing strips. They said that the most obvious manifestation in the town were the new cars—there was even a Porsche. Because of this trafficking activity, local consumption in the town had also increased. Similarly, in Santa

Cruz del Quiché, a group of adults noted that drug traffickers had been coming from the United States to sell cocaine to the local gangs; this was also a new phenomenon since the Peace Accords.

In terms of variations over shorter time frames people noted few marked variations. However, more drugs tended to be sold and consumed in the evenings after 10 o'clock and also during the weekends when people had more money to buy drugs. This also depended on the types of drugs consumed; those addicted to hard drugs took them all the time, while others who took them on a more recreational basis tended to do so when they went to local discos.

Types of Drugs Available

A variety of drugs were available in low-income communities. Overall, glue was the most common type of drug, followed by marijuana. However, this pattern was most common outside Guatemala City. In contrast, in communities in the capital, people tended to consume hard drugs such as cocaine, including crack cocaine, although marijuana was also very popular. When glue was not available, people sniffed paint thinner or white spirits available from hardware stores.

It is significant that many people were fully aware of the different types of drugs available. Figure 6.1, drawn by an 18-year-old man in Nuevo Horizonte, shows the types and usage of different drugs. In another example from La Merced, Guatemala City, a group of boys (aged between 10 and 12 years) were able to list the drugs they knew in their community.

In terms of the drug costs, some types were cheaper than alcohol. In Gucumatz, Santa Cruz del Quiché, for instance, a focus group of three young people reported that a cigarette of marijuana cost 30 *centavos*, compared with 2.25 *quetzales* for a bottle of soda.[1] Similarly, glue was only 25 centavos for a tube. Crack cocaine and cocaine were much more expensive at 300 *quetzales* for a stone of crack cocaine, and 100 *quetzales* for an ounce of cocaine. Indeed, a police official in Santa Cruz del Quiché reported that cocaine was mainly a drug for the middle and upper classes

Figure 6.1 Drawing of types of drugs available in Nueva Horizonte, Guatemala City (by an 18-year-old man)

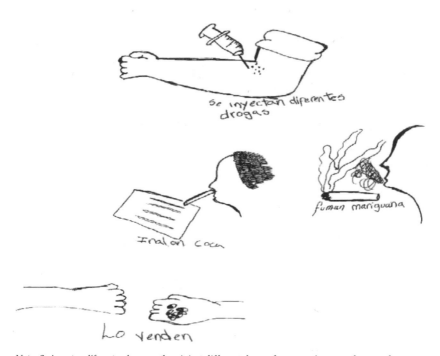

Note: Se inyectan diferentes drogas = they inject different drugs; *fuman mariguana* = they smoke marijuana; *inhalan coca* = they inhale cocaine; *lo venden* = they sell it.

in the region because of its expense. In La Merced, Guatemala City, drugs were much cheaper than in the peri-urban areas, which partly explains the higher rate of consumption. For instance, crack cocaine cost 15 *quetzales* per stone, while cocaine cost 25 *quetzales* per ounce. Nevertheless, drugs were generally still more expensive than alcohol in Guatemala City.

Characteristics of Drug Consumers

Drug consumption was associated with men rather than women, although in the Guatemala City communities women reported consuming drugs. In La Merced, Guatemala City, where drug consumption was widespread, a 40-year-old man estimated that about 10 percent of women in the *colonia* smoked marijuana. In terms of age, most drug addicts were young. A group of adolescent women in La Merced said that most drug addicts in the community were male (between 17 and 22 years old), who later, by the age of 30, became alcoholics. Another adult man, also from La Merced, said that if they didn't die first, people continued to take drugs until they were 50 because of addiction. He also suggested that the majority of youth in the community took drugs. Finally, a group of adult women reported that boys begin to sniff glue at the age of 10 and then moved on to marijuana at around age 15. After that they move on to harder drugs such as cocaine and crack cocaine. In Nuevo Horizonte, Guatemala City, a group of adults reported that boys as young as 11 were taking cocaine and crack cocaine.

Outside Guatemala City, levels of reported consumption were lower, with young men tending to start later, at around 15 years, and consuming mainly glue and marijuana. For example, in Villa Real, Esquipulas, a group of male adolescents stated that only 10 percent of the young men were involved in drug taking, while pointing out that some parents were clandestine glue sniffers. Similarly, in Limoncito, San Marcos, around 15 percent of the male youth in the community were said to be taking drugs, although they rarely took hard drugs, and in some cases the drugs taken were even referred to as traditional herbs and plants.

Causes of Drug Consumption

The perceived causes of drug consumption and addiction in communities were similar to those discussed in the case of alcoholism. However, the key difference was generational, with children and youth more likely than their parents to turn to drugs rather than to alcohol. This was identified as a continuum from fathers abusing alcohol, which in turn encouraged their sons to take drugs. In Figure 6.2, for instance, a couple from Villa Real, Esquipulas, explicitly identified alcoholism among parents as a cause of drug use among their sons.

As with alcohol, one of the most commonly mentioned causes of drug addiction was intrafamily violence and family disinte-

Figure 6.2 Causal impact diagram of drug addiction in Villa Real Esquipulas (prepared by a 35-year-old man and a 54-year-old woman)

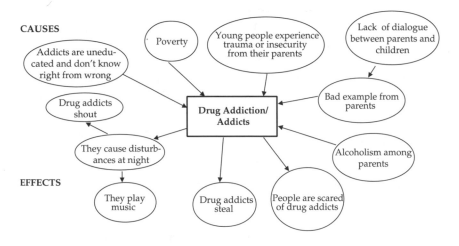

gration. This referred to the lack of love and communication between parents and children within families, as well as the lack of parental discipline of children.

In Sacuma, Huehuetenango, a group of four teachers identified all three factors as primary causes of drug addiction in their school, along with the influence of television and loss of moral values in society. Similarly, in figure 6.2, the Villa Real couple cited "lack of dialogue between parents and children" as a major cause of drug addiction. In some cases, causes were rooted in physical, sexual, and verbal abuse of children within the home. In Nuevo Horizonte, Guatemala City, three middle-aged women discussed the cause of drug addiction as "the bad example of the parents getting drunk and hitting them on a daily basis."

In all communities, mothers who "abandoned" their children to go out to work were cited as a reason for children's drug use. Left alone without discipline, children were easy prey for drug addicts and dealers recruiting new consumers. One woman in La Merced, Guatemala City, suggested that all drug addicts were originally abandoned children, either because their parents had separated, or because the mother went out to work, leaving the children alone.

Peer pressure and a desire to belong were also important among youth, especially when they suffered violence in the home, either as victims or witnesses. Knowledge of drugs meant that this easily became a way of dealing with problems. In Nuevo Horizonte, Guatemala City, two women at a women's group meeting pointed out: "Children begin to take drugs when they're young, they look at young men who do it, and then they want to do it as well." They went on to say that older people continued to take drugs because they are addicted. It should also be noted that some did take drugs as a recreational activity, as well as to deal with adverse circumstances.

In a few cases, poverty was also cited as a reason young people take drugs (figure 6.3), especially when they were unemployed. In these cases, they took drugs to pass the time or to forget about trying to get a job. In some cases young indigenous people reported that they turned to drugs when they felt discriminated against.

Some people, especially the elderly, blamed increased drug consumption in communities on increased drug sales and traf-

Figure 6.3 Causal impact diagram of drug consumption in Concepcíon, Guatemala City (prepared by five mothers)

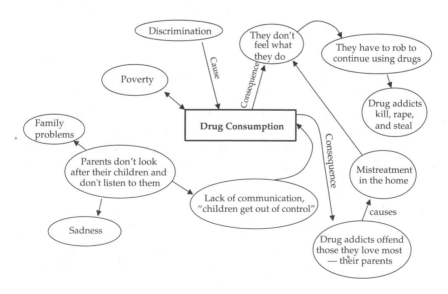

ficking at unprecedented levels. This was partly linked to increasing drugs on the market, but also related to drug consumers becoming "pushers" to feed their habit. In Sacuma, Huehuetenango, for instance, two women (aged 37 and 39) stated that young people started to deal because of ambition for power and money, and also because they could make "easy money." They also noted that this should be understood in light of the fact that few young people could secure very good jobs without turning to drug dealing.

Consequences of Drug Consumption

Drug consumption led to different types of violence, primarily economic in nature. The most common was robbery. To feed addictions drug users either committed burglaries or robbed individuals (figure 6.3). The latter usually involved assaults, muggings, and robbing wallets, handbags, and jewelry. Robbery on the part of drug addicts was also interrelated with delinquency and *mara* activity. In both cases, violence perpetrated by these groups was associated with drug consumption and sometimes drug sales and distribution (see chapter 7).

Drugs were also linked with sexual violence, especially rape. As five mothers from Concepción, Guatemala City, noted, "Drug addicts kill, rape, and steal." Two men from Nuevo Horizonte, Guatemala City, discussed how drug addicts were more likely to rape those girls who walked around the streets in "provocative" clothing; men under the influence of drugs, according to them, were less able to prevent themselves from raping. This was repeated many times, often in conjunction with the phrase: "They don't feel anything they're doing while taking drugs." Death was also discussed as a frequent outcome of drug taking, from illnesses, overdoses, or violence associated with drugs. In some cases, fighting over drugs and drug sale territories among *maras* within communities led to deaths of gang members, especially in Guatemala City.

Such consequences generated acute levels of fear of drugs within communities, weakening cognitive social capital. In Concepción, Guatemala City, an adult woman pointed out that "the drug addicts are a problem because when they're drugged they will do anything; they are violent and dangerous." People avoided certain parts of communities such as riverbanks, bridges, and cemeteries where drug addicts congregated. In Limoncito, San Marcos, for instance, everyone avoided the local cemetery in the evenings because of its association with drug addicts and, in turn, with *maras* and rapes.

In summary, it is important to emphasize that the drug problem in Guatemala, although in its infancy, has not really taken hold of communities outside Guatemala City. Having said this, it is still perceived as a major problem, although levels of drug use were often very low.

Note

1. There are 100 *centavos* in a *quetzal*.

7

The Violence of *Maras*, Robbers, and Delinquents

As poor urban communities struggle to rebuild in the post-conflict context of Guatemala the predominant problem articulated was the rapidly expanding presence of gangs (*maras*), robbers (*ladrones*), delinquents (*delincuentes*), and so-called loiterers (*vagancia*) (tables 7.1 and 7.2).

As four young women (aged between 15–17) in Nuevo Horizonte, Guatemala City, so aptly stated, "The *maras* and robbers are always the principal problem; we lack money because they make assaults in the street and on the passenger buses."

The Nature and Scope of Violence Related to Gangs, Robbers, and Delinquents

When focus groups specifically listed different types of violence that were a problem, gangs, thieves, and delinquents dominated economic violence (table 7.2). Together, these three types of violence constituted the most important category, representing almost half of the violence identified in all nine communities (46 percent). In addition, much of the rape outside the home identified as social violence (constituting 8 percent of all violence) was attributed to gangs.

Within such a broad category it was difficult to distinguish between different subcategories, particularly as the term *maras*

Table 7.1   Gang-, robber-, and delinquent-related violence
as a proportion of all violence-related problems

Community	Violence-related problem as a proportion of general problems	Gang-, robber-, delinquent-related violence as a proportion of violence-related problems
Concepción, Guatemala City	54	55
Nuevo Horizonte, Guatemala City	51	45
La Merced, Guatemala City	46	63
Sacuma, Huehuetenango	60	60
Limoncito, San Marcos	49	42
El Carmen, Santa Lucía, Cotzumalguapa	47	57
Villa Real, Esquipulas	36	63
Gucumatz, Santa Cruz del Quiché	51	43
San Jorge, Chinautla	33	42
Total	48	55

Source: 199 Listings of general problems.

increasingly had become a catchall term for male street violence.
Listings of general problems and types of violence demonstrated
a large number of overlapping categories (box 7.1).

Robbers or gangs were often perceived as either synonymous,
or as very closely causally interrelated. For instance, in La Merced,
Guatemala City, a focus group of elderly people identified robbers and gangs as the same. In Sacuma, Huehuetenango, a group
of 11 indigenous women drew a diagram to show the compli-
cated links among gangs, delinquents, and drugs. They also identified the consequences of gangs, delinquents, and drugs in terms
of other problems manifested (figure 7.1). Figure 7.2, drawn by a
12-year-old boy, illustrates yet another categorization of different types of gangs.

On closer examination, however, a useful distinction was
made in this seemingly heterogeneous group of social actors,
based on two criteria in particular: first, the type of violence per-

Table 7.2 Types of economic violence perpetrated by gangs, delinquents, and robbers in nine communities (*as percentage of economic, social, and political violence*)

Community					Type of economic violence					
	Drugs	Inse-curity	Robbery/ assault	Delin-quency	Loiter-ing	Maras/ gangs	Prosti-tution	Kidnap-ping	Armed attacks	Total
Concepción, Guatemala City	12	1	11	3	—	5	1	3	8	**44**
Nuevo Hirozonte, Guatemala City	8	—	11	7	1	6	2	2	2	**39**
La Merced, Guatemala City	12	—	12	3	1	19	—	1	10	**58**
Sacuma, Huehuetenango	12	3	5	3	—	11	—	11	3	**48**
Limoncito, San Marcos	15	3	18	5	—	18	—	—	—	**59**
El Carmen, Santa Lucía, Cotzumalguapa	10	—	22	2	2	10	4	—	2	**52**
Villa Real, Esquipulas	—	2	6	1	—	18	—	2	11	**40**
Gucumatz, Santa Cruz del Quiché	12	1	18	5	5	6	2	6	—	**55**
San Jorge, Chinautla	6	1	4	—	—	9	—	—	1	**21**
Total	**10**	**1**	**12**	**3**	**1**	**11**	**3**	**3**	**4**	**46**

Source: 154 listings of violence.

Box 7.1   Types of gang-, robber-, and delinquent-related violence

Maras	*Maras'* abuse of women
Robbers	Delinquency
Assaults	Kidnapping
Loiterers	Assassinations
Fights	Violence between men
Street violence	Dangerous places
Thieves	Killing fights
Young people who	*Pandillas*
make problems	Danger in the streets
Problems with youth	Young men who go around
Youth who insult	upsetting people
Cholos who disturb	Gang fights—to the death
Fights at night	Danger in the streets
Guerrillas	People with guns
Maras who paint the walls	*Maras* killing people
Actions between *maras*	*Maras* breaking windows

Note: Maras—Specific Central American term for gangs
Cholos—Slang term for *maras*; literally means "mixed race"
Pandillas—Common Latin American term for gang
Source: 199 Listings of general problems and types of violence in nine communities.

---

petrated; and second, whether or not the actors were also members of a social institution.

In terms of these criteria, robbers, delinquents, and loiterers were very generally categorized together on the basis that they all perpetrated economic violence—with their motive economic gain. They could also be categorized on the basis that generally they were not formally, or even informally, members of a specific group or social institution—although a group might join together to undertake a particular robbery or other act of violence.

In contrast, *maras* formed a separate distinct category on two counts. First, in addition to robbery and assault, they were attributed as primarily involved in other distinct forms of violence

**Figure 7.1   Causal impact diagram of relationships between
different types of violence in Sacuma, Huehuetenango (identified
by a group of indigenous women aged 22–46)**

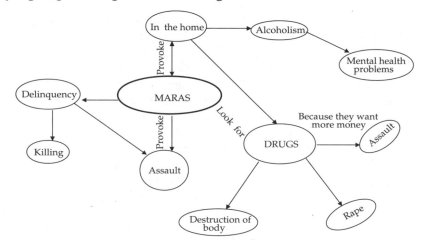

including physical fighting with other gangs and rape of women
and young girls—neither of which were primarily economic in
motive. Second, and more important, they were members of a
distinct, widely recognized, social institution. This distinction was
clearly identified by, for instance, the deputy chief of the police
station in La Merced, Guatemala City, when he drew a diagram
of causal relationships of different types of violence (figure 7.3).
He identified the linkages between common delinquents and
gangs, and also the differences between delinquents who rob and
gangs who also fight among each other. For this reason the following section focuses separately on these two subgroups, while
recognizing the close interrelationships between them. Equally,
because the *mara* is a very specific Central American phenomenon, the study uses this term throughout.

The Phenomenon of the *Maras*

Description of Maras

In all the nine communities focus groups perceived *maras* as having a number of similar, clearly defined characteristics (table 7.3).

Figure 7.2 Drawing of different types of gangs in La Merced, Guatemala City (by a 12-year-old boy)

Note: ladron – robber; *cholos* = type of gang influenced by U.S. fashion; *marero* = *mara*/gang member; *pandillas* = type of gang.

Figure 7.3 Diagram of linkages between delinquency and *maras* in La Merced, Guatemala City (identified by deputy chief of local police station)

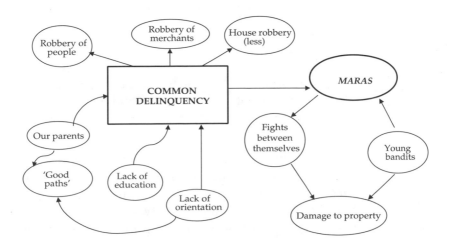

Table 7.3   Descriptive information on *maras* from focus groups in seven communities

Community	Descriptive information on numbers and names of maras
La Merced, Guatemala City	First established in 1989. Gangs include La 13, La 18, Picapiedras, White Fence (WF), Maras Salvatruchas (MS), and Latin King (LK), of which four are predominant in the area.
Sacuma, Huehuetenango	30 groups in total in Huehuetenango; three in Sacuma.
Limoncito, San Marcos	First established in 1990; called 18, 13, Los Cholos, Pirana, Los del Tope, Los Duendes Metalicos.
El Carmen, Santa Lucía, Cotzumalguapa	Described as *cholos*; Salvatruchas (from El Salvador) and La 13 and La 18 from the United States: identified as well organized.
Villa Real, Esquipulas	Some are known as *grupos satanicos* (satanic groups); 10–15 percent were women's *maras*.
Gucumatz, Santa Cruz del Quiché	AVQ (*Asociación de Vagos Quichenses*)—more than 100 members and most important gang; Bichos, BN (Barrio Norte)—more than 50 members; Cachudos, 13, 18, MS, Las Chicas Big—more than 15 members; Las Chicas—new; Calambres—more than 20 members; Salvatruchas, Cholos, Escorpion, Lenguas, Los Duendes—more than 20 members.
San Jorge, Chinautla	Established in 1990; three to four groups in area including Satan, Escorpiones, and Salvatruchas.

Most important, they were a widespread phenomenon. On average, between three and four groups of *maras* existed in each of the communities in which the appraisal was undertaken. As a young woman in La Merced, Guatemala City, stated, "The community is full of *maras*. All the youth are integrated into the *maras* simply for solidarity." In addition, the number of youth joining the *maras* and the number of the groups themselves had increased fundamentally during the past decade and was very much a phenomenon of the 1990s. In La Merced, Guatemala City, for instance, the *maras* first came into the area in 1989, and 1999 was the year of greatest proliferation. On the other side of Guatemala, in Limoncito, San Marcos, focus groups identified the *maras* as first forming in 1990 (table 7.3).

All the *maras* had specific characteristics in terms of their clothing, tattoos, and identity. Most common were the large baggy denim trousers that gave *maras* the nickname of *cholos*. In addition, strict adherence to particular color combinations in clothing was important. In La Merced, Guatemala City, for instance, three out of four groups wore red and white clothing. Finally, *maras* were closely linked to the "ownership," control, and defense of physical space within communities. Related to this territoriality, conflict between gangs was a critical component of gang life with groups often forming and reforming alliances among themselves. In La Merced, Guatemala City, there were four main groups, and each controlled a different spatial area. While fights to maintain turf occurred, so too did collaboration between different groups as depicted by three young men who were members of *maras* that drew figure 7.4. A mother and her daughter in Sacuma, Huehuetenango, included both gangs and vengeance in a list of violence problems, stating, "There is vengeance between *maras*, they fight between themselves. If one does something against the *maras* they take revenge."

Variations and Causes of Mara Activity

The causes of the phenomenon of the *maras*, and the associated reasons for joining, varied widely. This related not only to regional location, but also, and more importantly, to the function of the group and the associated age and gender of its members. In addition, perceptions varied among focus groups particularly depending on their age and whether they were themselves members of the *maras*. As social institutions *maras* formed a continuum. At one end, young people considered them to be informal groups

Figure 7.4 Diagram of collaboration among *mara* groups in La Merced, Guatemala City (drawn by three young men who were members of *maras* aged 18–20)

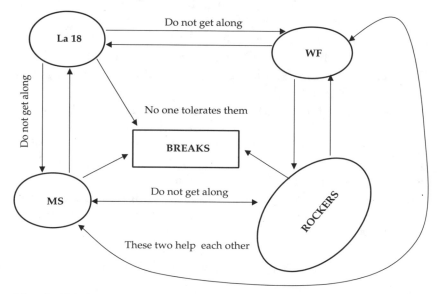

Note: La 18, MS, WF, and Rockers are all the names of local *maras*.

that provided youth cultural identity and mutual support for young urban adolescents. At the other end of the continuum, people—particularly older people—described the *maras* as dangerous robbers, drug addicts, and killers. In the latter case they sometimes substituted the word *bandas* (literally bands) for *maras*. For instance, in Santa Cruz del Quiché one group based the distinction between *maras* and *bandas* on the fact that *maras* join together to amuse themselves, while *bandas* are armed. In other cases, such as in Villa Real, Esquipulas; and Limoncito, San Marcos, the word *pandillas* (literal term for gangs) was also on occasion substituted for *maras*.

Although informal groups of boys and young men have long been associated with the process of reaching male adulthood in urban areas, the *maras* as a Central American phenomenon have accelerated rapidly in the past decade. They were closely linked to external influences and the "phenomenon of imitation," as defined by an elderly man in Limoncito, San Marcos. This related particularly to the post-conflict return-migration of many individuals and their families from other Central American countries such as El Salvador and Honduras, as well as from the United States. In addition, it was one of a number of consequences of globalization, in terms of the transnational transfer of influence of violent movies, designer and sport clothing, and popular rap and rock music.

Both the *maras* called La 18 and the Salvatruchas, which were common in many of the research communities (table 7.3), had their origins in El Salvador. In some cases their leaders came from El Salvador or the United States to form the *mara* group in Guatemala. In La Merced, Guatemala City, the White Fence (WF), LK (Latin King) and La 18 had the same names as gangs in Los Angeles, California, with youth returning from the United States bringing their gang experience back with them to Guatemala, often after having been deported. A focus group of an elderly couple and their eldest son in Sacuma, Huehuetenango, stated, "The *maras* are not from here, they come from over there, they are Salvadorian by their clothing." In Villa Real, Esquipulas, in eastern Guatemala, a local shop owner said that the *maras* came from El Salvador and Honduras. They were young men who wanted to go to the United States, who, when they could not get through, or could not find a guide (*coyote*) to the United States, remained in Esquipulas forming *maras*.

The increase in the *maras* was not only associated with external influences, but in some parts of the country with the peace process itself. In Sacuma, Huehuetenango, an area of the country seriously affected by the civil war, a group of six women described how they perceived the importance of the *maras* had increased (figure 7.5). Of particular relevance for them was that they considered the maras to be signing accords of violence at the same time that the Peace Accords were signed in 1996.

A young 16-year-old female named Cristina, from La Merced, Guatemala City, although not a member herself, described the different stages in the process of joining the *maras* (figure 7.6) on the basis of her knowledge gained through her friends who belonged to *maras*. On the one hand, she said that joining *maras* was part of growing up:

Figure 7.5   Timeline of changing levels of *mara* activity in Sacuma, Huehuetenango (according to six women aged 30–60)

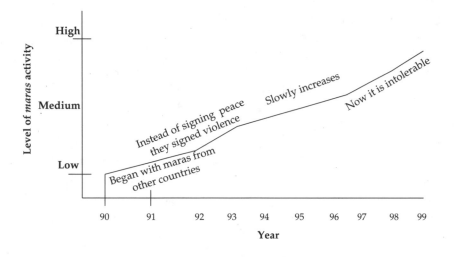

It's a way of being a young man. Male youth begin drinking with their friends, go to discotheques and in this way get to know members of *maras*. But those who actually join *maras* are more likely to be young boys who have suffered at home and been badly treated by their fathers. The effects of this are very serious. The youth first get involved in drugs, rob to service their habit, families no longer want them as they rob them, and as a result are rejected by the whole community.

Although primarily a male social institution, in some contexts a small number of female *maras* also existed. Cristina also explained that girls joined *maras* for very different reasons from those of men. One of the principal reasons for joining was to acquire a boyfriend or fiancé. However, when their fathers at home mistreat girls, their friends encouraged them to leave home and join a *mara* that could protect them from this mistreatment. In some cases "It's better to be with the *mara* than with the family," as Cristina stated. Some girl *mara* members get involved in drugs

Figure 7.6 Causal impact diagram of the causes and effects of being a male and female gang member in La Merced, Guatemala City (drawn by a young girl aged 16)

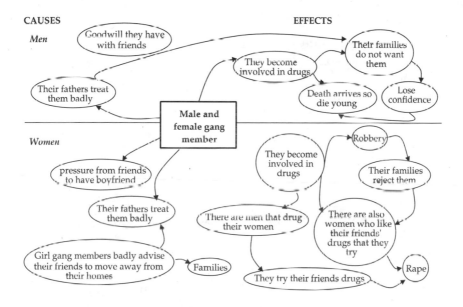

for pleasure, while others are forced into drugs by their boyfriends "who take advantage of them."

Mistreatment at home, as described by Cristina, was the most commonly cited cause of joining the *maras* in all communities. A 39-year-old carpenter in Villa Real, Esquipulas, said that youth joined the *maras* because their fathers did not give their sons attention, and consequently there was "little communication between them." Two middle-aged women in the same community explained that the lack of communication meant that parents did not have time for their sons; consequently, young people looked for confidence and a better life outside their homes. In Concepción, Guatemala City, five women health workers in the local health center cited "rejection by parents" and "lack of education in the family" as the two main reasons for joining a *mara*. In San Jorge, Chinautla, one of the members of a group of four young people said: "Children grow up without love so they stay in the streets and look for love from the *maras*; what their families don't give them, the *maras* do."

A group of indigenous women of mixed ages in Gucumatz, Santa Cruz del Quiché, listed lack of relationship between parents, lack of respect of society, and badly brought up children as three causes for joining the *maras*. This was also linked to a decline in respect for their parents on the part of the younger generation.

Associated with mistreatment at home was the bad example provided by parents. An elderly man who worked in the mayor's office in Limoncito, San Marcos, described how his 14-year-old grandson was a member of the *maras* because of the bad example of his parents. His father smoked marijuana and his mother was an alcoholic, and the young boy himself was also addicted to marijuana. Don José was highly concerned about the grave consequences of being a member of the *maras* that could result in his grandson ending up in hospital or even the cemetery. Equally important was the "breakdown" of the family caused by divorce or separation—often caused by fathers coming home drunk and beating up their mothers—with families disintegrating and children not knowing to whom to turn. Figure 7.7 provides a comprehensive summary of many of the family-related causal factors as identified by three schoolteachers in Sacuma, Huehuetenango.

Another reason for joining *maras* related to conflicts among both children and youth at school. In Gucumatz, Santa Cruz del Quiché, three young indigenous women (aged 14–20) described the general tendencies in terms of youth joining the *mara* (figure 7.8). Youths from 10 to 12 years often joined the *maras* because they have problems with companions at school, and older members of the *maras* will defend them. The majority joined between 13–16 years because of the attraction of the fashion in clothing and music associated with *maras*. The older *maras* of 18–20 years, and on occasions even older, committed assault and were dangerous. A 14-year-old schoolboy from La Merced, Guatemala City, identified that there were only two ways of leaving the *maras*: either by marrying or by leaving the community. An elderly woman from the same community recounted how each of her three sons had been a member of the *maras* as a normal part of

Figure 7.7 Problem tree of causes and effects of *maras* in Sacuma, Huehuetenango (drawn by a group of three primary school teachers aged 20–40)

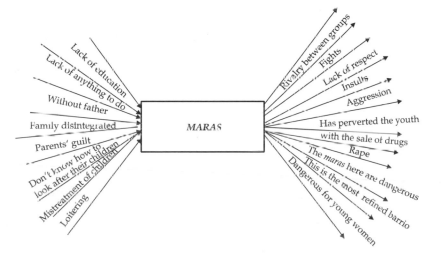

the process of growing up in the community. But, as each in turn had found a girlfriend, settled down with a regular job, and had children, they had systematically left the *maras*.

In some cases, as noted earlier, there were female-only maras. A mixed group of indigenous people from Gucumatz, Santa Cruz del Quiché, comprising a 14-year-old boy and two young women aged 15 and 26, explained that among the indigenous population in their community there were two groups of girl *maras*. These were young adolescent girls who had abandoned their traditional *traje* (costume) for large trousers, they were all the girlfriends of members of male *maras*, and many had become pregnant. Of the two groups identified, *Las Chicas Big* (literally the Big Girls), had more than 20 members and were the girlfriends of members of the male gang called *Los Calambres*, while the other, *Las Chicas* (the Girls), were female gang members in their own right.

Again, the strong desire of young people to join the *maras* because of their association with U.S.-influenced youth culture was a widely reflected theme. In Gucumatz, Santa Cruz del Quiché, the same group identified the following three reasons for joining the *maras*: for the music—rap and rock that "allows

Figure 7.8 Timeline on age of joining the *maras* in Gucumatz, Santa Cruz del Quiché (identified by three women aged 14–20)

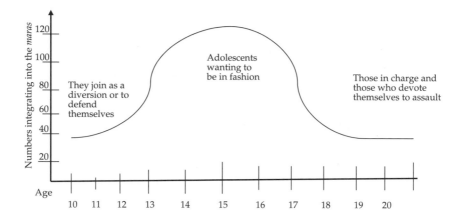

much violence"; for the wardrobe—for the fashion; and, finally "for respect." Again, they also mentioned that if a youngster has a fight at school he could call on an older *mara* member to defend him.

Consequences of the Maras

Consequences of the *mara* phenomenon depended on the perceptions of different social actors. For the *maras* themselves such institutions provided important support structures, solidarity, and a mechanism for group identity in a difficult and changing world. As one young *mara* member in La Merced, Guatemala City, stated, "Belonging to the *maras* means I have friends to help me, loan me money, and provide activities on the weekends." This was corroborated by two young men in the same community who confirmed the importance of *maras* for local youth in terms of providing leisure pursuits for the weekend. They maintained that, since the majority of *maras* either attended school or were in some type of employment during the week, maximum activity occurred at the weekend when they had more free time.

However, for others in the communities the impact of the *maras* had become more serious. As noted earlier, it is important to disaggregate between different types of *maras*, by age and location. Three schoolteachers in Sacuma, Huehuetenango, who were concerned about the impact of *maras* in school, for instance, identified a range of consequences at the individual and community level (figure 7.9). These ranged from practical constraints relating to reducing mobility for studying at night—with impact on human capital—to more serious issues such as the breakdown of order when authorities lacked control over the *maras*—in this case with implications for community-level social capital. The fact that the police were afraid of the *maras* was also identified by focus groups in other communities such as Limoncito, San Marcos.

Another group of teachers in San Jorge, Chinautla, (a mixed group of five indigenous and *ladinos*) identified gratuitous and unprovoked damage to local community facilities caused by *maras*, attacking the local school and breaking windows and painting the walls with graffiti—showing its impact on human capital. The group claimed that there was nothing they themselves

Figure 7.9 Causal impact diagram of *maras* in Sacuma, Huehuetenango (identified by three primary schoolteachers aged 20–35)

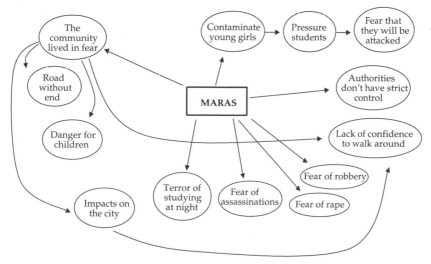

could do. They did not know the individuals concerned (although they knew the group of *maras* that had perpetrated the crimes), but more importantly they feared reprisal.

Across communities *maras* caused irritation by painting walls to mark their presence in their territory. The aim of this was to intimidate people by walking around the streets shouting and swearing, and disrupting dances and other local events by fighting between different groups while drinking heavily. Adults and the elderly were the most concerned with these activities, causing widespread intergenerational tension. Figure 7.10 shows the perception of two young men in La Merced, Guatemala City. They described the manner in which groups of *maras* start on *broncas* (fights) during the weekends—either among themselves or with gangs in neighboring communities.

The range of activities described by a group of young people in Gucumatz, Santa Cruz del Quiché (box 7.2), is representative of more serious problems associated with some of the *maras* across all communities. They closely associated *maras* with drugs and alcohol. In many communities this was linked to selling drugs and introducing drugs to schoolchildren and young people.

Figure 7.10 Timeline of weekly activities of *maras* in La Merced, Guatemala City (according to two men aged 20–24)

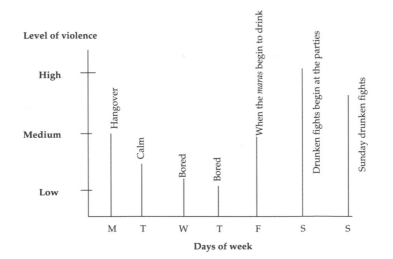

Box 7.2   Activities of *maras* in Gucumatz, Santa Cruz del Quiché (identified by a mixed group of nine young people (aged 14–20)

- Drink alcohol
- Look for problems with other *maras*—to see who is the better *mara*
- Fight with other *maras* for girlfriends or for vengeance
- Paint walls with graffiti—to let people know who they are, mark their territory, and insult other *maras*
- Consume drugs—when they have money (including paint thinner, glue, cocaine, and marijuana)
- Rob when necessary
- Traffic in drugs
- Attend dances where they start fights with other gangs

Equally serious was revenge fighting between gangs, which on occasion resulted in killings. In Gucumatz, Santa Cruz del Quiché, a group of four *ladinos* (three men and one woman, aged between 22–40) said that assaults and killings between *maras* were destabilizing the peace process. Rivalry between different *maras* was not only based on territorial disputes. A group of 17- to 22-year-old young men in La Merced described how it was also the consequence of differences of opinion over types of music (rap or rock), rivalry for particular young women in the community, and amounts of alcohol consumed.

Most grave was the association of *maras* with the rape of young women, particularly when the perpetrators were high on drugs or inebriated by alcohol. A 22-year-old woman in San Jorge, Chinautla, described that "they fight among themselves using knives and machetes and threaten girls because they are pretty and they want to rape them." In Villa Real, Esquipulas, a group of young women, reluctant to be specific, stated that "the principal problem for men was they beat them, and to women they did other things." In San Jorge, Chinautla, two men identified as members of the *maras* had recently raped a 14-year-old girl. This violent act was reported by numerous focus groups including four school-aged adolescents, a group of teachers, and three girls aged 14–19—demonstrating the gravity with which the incident was viewed.

In totality, the increasingly widespread presence of *maras* in all the communities studied exacerbated levels of fear felt by the community members. Associated with this was a reduction in people's mobility, both within the community and outside it, particularly at night. As two women from Nuevo Horizonte, Guatemala City, said, "People cannot walk in safety, you do not go out in tranquility." A group of male workers in a ceramic artisan workshop in San Jorge, Chinautla, confirmed that because of the *maras*, "there is fear of going out at night and on Saturdays," sentiments echoed elsewhere in Santa Cruz del Quiché and San Marcos. Five female health workers in Concepción, Guatemala City, identified *maras* as a source of severe area stigma for their community; they stated that because of the *maras'* presence in their community people from outside the neighborhood no longer visited them, and they could no longer get credit from banks.

This reduction in mobility had important implications at individual and community levels. Many young people were not able to participate in evening educational activities, and community groups who might have met after work hours were unable to do so—thus affecting community-level social capital (see chapter 8).

The Phenomena of Robbery and Delinquency

Description of Robbers and Delinquents

There were differences as well as similarities between *maras*, robbers, and delinquents. In addition, there were differences within the latter category, despite a tendency for community members to speak of them interchangeably. Delinquents were most commonly boys and young men who had dropped out of school and who hung around on street corners. Out of boredom, forced idleness, and consumption of less serious drugs such as marijuana, they were often involved in petty crimes such as snatching handbags or shoplifting.

Robbers, in contrast, were more likely to be older in age, more serious criminals, far more violent in nature, and often associated with assault. As one elderly woman in Villa Real, Esquipulas, stated: "They (robbers) bother us a lot in the community. They rob everything, even shoes." Most communities identified that the phenomenon of individual robbery had existed since the establishment of the community. However, more recently robberies took place not only in private homes, but also in public areas, such as attacks on people and trucks, theft from local street markets, and, in some areas of the country, kidnapping for financial extortion. A less obvious type of economic violence was that of bus drivers fighting among themselves to get passengers. As illustrated in table 7.2, robbery (the largest single category of economic violence), together with armed attacks and kidnapping, represented 19 percent of the 46 percent of economic violence (expressed as a percentage of total economic, social, and political violence) perpetrated by gangs, delinquents, and robbers in the communities studied.

Variations and Causes of Robbery and Delinquency

Many groups in the nine communities considered that delinquency was the outcome of a lack of adequate parental care. A 30-year-old woman in La Merced, Guatemala City, for instance, identified a variety of factors including parental irresponsibility, neglect because of vices such as alcohol, and the fact that many working parents left their children on their own at home. This affected the children in a number of ways. Some did not want to study and so dropped out of school; others were afraid when left on their own at home; while still others were left without food. All of these were important reasons for children to spend their days wandering around the community and loitering on street corners.

Robbery was associated primarily with lack of employment, and here the causes varied. Older people, in particular, cited an unwillingness to work as a reason for stealing, while younger people were more likely to associate this with the inability to find work. A 26-year-old woman shopkeeper in Villa Real (a single mother whose husband had migrated to the United States) commented, "There are no sources of work for young people so they become robbers; however, there are also young people who want an easy life." A group of five youths in Nuevo Horizonte, Guatemala City, identified the causes of robbery as a combination of lack of work, laziness, and lack of study (figure 7.11).

In Limoncito, San Marcos, timelines showed the relationship between robbery and different employment strategies. A group of three women (aged 22–61 years) highlighted differences in the level of robbery over both the weekly and monthly periods. There were more robberies around the fifteenth and thirty-first of each month when workers received their pay packets and "were walking around with money." In a context where many of the male wage earners worked during the week in Guatemala City (five hours' bus ride away) returning home only on weekends, robberies were highest on Sunday afternoons and Mondays. This was when the men had returned to the city, and "the women were making their purchases with the money their husbands had left them" (figure 7.12).

Figure 7.11 Causal impact diagram of causes and effect of robbery in Nuevo Horizonte, Guatemala City (drawn by five youths aged 14–16)

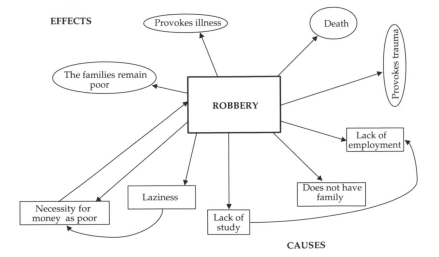

In both La Merced, Guatemala City, and San Jorge, Chinautla, different groups of young women (aged 8–15 and 14–19, respectively) identified *Semana Santa* (Easter Week in March/April) and Christmas (December) as times for peak robbery activity. Not only did robbers want to acquire goods themselves, but people had more money at this time or had left their homes empty to celebrate with family in other parts of the country.

In some areas robbery was closely linked to the annual agricultural cycle. According to a group of four young men in El Carmen, Cotzumalguapa, scarcity of work when the harvest (*zafra*) finished meant that men were so desperate that they robbed. A second mixed group (aged 22–25) complemented this with the information that May to November was the period of the highest incidence of robbery "because the sugar refineries do

Figure 7.12 Timelines of robber activity in Limoncito, San Marcos (drawn by a group of three women aged 22–61)

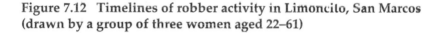
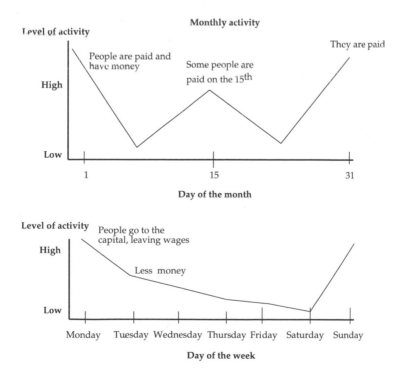

not have activities and consequently there is no work for many people." Another group of six young men (aged 20–35) from the same community linked this to the fact that lots of foreigners from El Salvador and Honduras had come to the community. Groups in this community specifically listed kidnapping as a form of violent robbery. A group of three adults (aged 40–72) associated kidnapping with out-of-work agricultural workers at loose ends once the harvest was completed.

Some communities identified a decline in robbery. In Nuevo Horizonte, Guatemala City, a middle-aged couple commented that lack of employment had been the main cause of robbery, but this had declined, first, because some members of the community had taken justice into their own hands and had killed identified perpetrators. Second, and more recently, increases in employment had led to a decline in robbery.

Above all, changes in levels of robbery were also closely linked to changes in the police force, and here perceptions differed across communities depending on whether or not the new *Policia Nacional Civil* (National Civil Police) had been introduced. In El Merced, Guatemala City, for instance, an elderly couple summarized their perception of the changes as follows (figure 7.13). Between 1980 and 1995 the numbers of robbers had increased along with their increasing lack of fear of the policing system. However, following the Peace Accords in 1996 everything had changed. The new *Policia Nacional Civil* had been introduced into the community and this had assisted in reducing the level of robbery. Interestingly enough, in the same community, community members did not necessarily agree that the *Policia Nacional Civil* had had the same impact on the levels of *mara* activity.

Consequences of Robbery and Delinquency

The presence of a large number of robbers and delinquents was similar in impact to that of the *maras*. It increased levels of fear and reduced mobility, particularly at night. However, because of the specifically economic nature of the violence, it had several specific economic consequences. A group of six highschool boys in San Jorge, Chinautla, felt that robbery most affected the poor-

Figure 7.13   Timeline of changes in robbers' activity between 1980 and 1999 in La Merced, Guatemala City (drawn by an elderly couple aged 64 to 70)

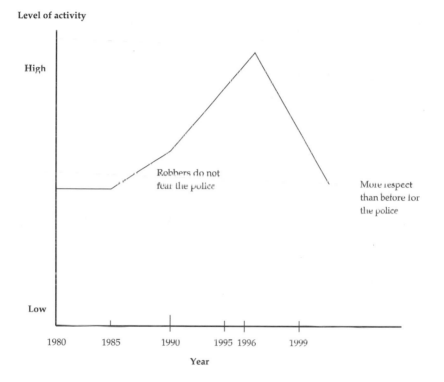

Level of activity

High

Robbers do not
fear the police

More respect
than before for
the police

Low

1980   1985   1990   1995 1996   1999

Year

est in the community. They could not defend themselves because their houses were built of corrugated iron sheets. In Villa Real, Esquipulas, the diagram drawn by a woman (figure 7.14), highlighted the fear felt, while also identifying the consequences for the robbers themselves. The consequences for robbers were prison, as well as the possibility of people taking the law into their own hands and killing the robbers (lynching).

In El Carmen, Santa Lucía Cotzumalguapa, a group of six men (aged 20–35) distinguished between *maras* and robbers. They agreed that the large number of robbers had affected the reputation and image of the community, creating area stigma. This had resulted in a reduction in the number of tourists to the area: "Tourists do not like to come because they are robbed. Before, they

Figure 7.14 The causes and effects of robbers in Villa Real, Esquipulas (drawn by an adult woman aged 26)

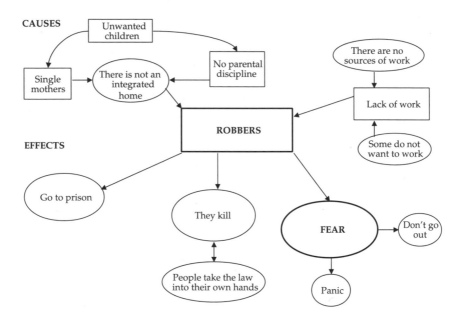

came to see the *piedras* [literally the stones but referring to the prehistoric stone carvings], but there they were grabbed [by robbers]."

While the study showed that *maras*, robbers, and delinquents all had adverse impacts on communities, perceptions from different members in the nine communities showed the importance of not making sweeping generalizations about them. Young male *maras* viewed the gangs as important positive social institutions. Other groups, however, viewed them negatively because they were responsible for eroding human and social capital in communities. Similarities and differences among *maras*, robbers, and delinquents all highlighted the context-specific complexity of such groups.

8

Community-level Social Institutions and Perverse and Productive Social Capital

Violence not only affects individuals and households but also communities themselves through its impact on particular social institutions and their associated social capital. Structural social capital, the main focus here, refers to interpersonal relationships in formal or informal organizations or networks. Cognitive social capital refers to values, norms, attitudes, and beliefs that exist among neighbors, friends, and relatives at the community level. The two kinds of social capital are intricately linked; structural and cognitive social capital can be identified along a continuum from the societal to local to individual levels (Uphoff 1997).

Prevalence and Importance of Social Institutions

Community members identified 322 social institutions in the nine research communities studied (table 8.1). The total number of institutions identified was used as a proxy for perceptions of the *prevalence* of social institutions. The number of times an institution was cited was used as a proxy for perceptions of its *importance* (Groothaert 1998, 1999). Institutions were also classified according to their membership, ownership, and decisionmaking control. The study distinguished between membership groups in which people participated, either formally or informally, in

Table 8.1 Prevalence of social institutions by type (*percent of total number of institutions*)

Type of institution	Concepción, Guatemala City	Nuevo Horizonte, Guatemala City	La Merced, Guatemala City	San Jorge, Chinautla	Sacuma, Huehuetenango	Limoncito, San Marcos	Villa Real, Esquipulas	Gucumatz, Santa Cruz del Quiché	El Carmen, Santa Lucía Cotzumalguapa	Total
Membership Organizations										
Religious groups	2	5	2	6	2	7	3	2	8	37 (44)
Neighborhood committees	3	3	3	0	1	2	3	1	2	18 (21.4)
Violence-related groups	0	1	3	2	1	2	2	0	0	11 (13.1)
Youth, sports, and recreational organizations	2	3	3	0	2	0	0	1	0	11 (13.1)
Women's and childcare organizations	0	2	2	0	0	0	0	2	0	6 (7.1)
Organizations for the elderly	0	0	0	0	0	0	0	1	0	1 (1.2)
Subtotal	7	14	13	8	6	11	8	7	10	84
Service Delivery Organizations										
Social service organizations	2	12	9	7	9	10	1	8	10	68 (28.6)
NGOs	4	12	7	5	1	2	3	23	5	62 (26)
State/government organizations	2	0	4	5	2	1	1	21	5	41 (17.2)

Productive service organizations	1	2	0	1	2	9	1	10	5	31 (13)
State security/ justice institutions	0	1	2	0	2	1	2	5	5	18 (7.6)
Drug/alcohol rehab- ilitation centers	2	1	0	1	1	1	3	1	2	12 (5)
Private sector organizations	0	0	0	1	5	0	0	0	0	6 (2.5)
Subtotal	11	28	22	20	22	24	11	68	32	238
Total	**18**	**42**	**35**	**28**	**28**	**35**	**19**	**75**	**42**	**322**

Notes: Figures in parentheses represent percent of total. The category of religious groups refers to churches and prayer groups only. Religious organizations that provide social services are included in the appropriate service delivery category.

Source: 126 institutional listings, institutional mapping/Venn diagrams, and institutional preference matrixes from focus groups.

the functioning of the organizations, and service delivery organizations, in which community members did not make decisions.[1]

In terms of the prevalence of institutions, the largest single type was those providing social services (mainly schools and health centers). While some were privately run, most were owned and run by the government. Thus the state played an extremely important role in the institutional make-up of communities. The second most prevalent type was NGOs, followed by state/government institutions and the church (both Roman Catholic and evangelical) (table 8.1).

Violence-related organizations were only identified in a minority of cases. Although the *maras* emerged as a significant problem within communities, people tended not to view them as institutions. However, there were as many violence-related organizations as there were youth, sports, and recreational organizations (table 8.1).

Prevalence patterns varied according to community, ranging from only 18 institutions identified in Concepción, Guatemala City, to 75 in Gucumatz, Santa Cruz del Quiché. In Quiché, almost one-third of all the institutions were NGOs—the highest of all communities—with another third state institutions. This related to the influx of organizations and social movements in the aftermath of the civil war, many linked to the indigenous movement. There were also more NGOs in communities in Guatemala City and nearby Chinautla than in communities in more remote departmental capitals, such as Huehuetenango and San Marcos.

Service delivery organizations were significantly more prevalent than membership organizations. Just over one-quarter of all institutions involved membership (26.1 percent), compared with almost three-quarters that delivered services (73.9 percent). Religious organizations were the most prevalent membership groups in communities (44 percent), with social services and NGOs the most significant types of service deliverers (table 8.1).

Differences among communities highlighted the low proportions of membership organizations (table 8.1) in Gucumatz, Santa Cruz del Quiché (9.3 percent of the total), and in Sacuma, Huehuetenango (21.4 percent)—both departments previously affected by the civil conflict and with high component indigenous populations. In contrast, communities in Guatemala City and Villa Real, Esquipulas, had higher than average proportions of membership organizations.

Similar patterns emerged in terms of the importance of institutions, with social service delivery organizations perceived as most important, followed by NGOs, which were particularly important for indigenous groups. The church and religious groups were also important, representing almost half of all membership organizations (table 8.2).

Trust in Social Institutions

Community members were asked to indicate whether they viewed each institution positively (interpreted as indicating a high level of trust) or negatively (interpreted as indicating a low level of trust). Among membership organizations, youth, sports, and recreation groups received the highest percentage of positive rankings (82 percent).[2] Drug and alcohol rehabilitation centers—primarily Alcoholics Anonymous—received the highest percentage of positive rankings for service delivery organizations. Also receiving high percentages were religious groups (79 percent) and women's and childcare organizations (76 percent). (See table 8.3.)

From a negative perspective, lack of trust in state and government institutions was marked, prevalent among *ladino* and indigenous groups but particularly notable among the latter. State security and justice organizations such as the police and army received the highest percentage of negative rankings among service delivery institutions (61 percent), while the least trusted membership organizations were those associated with the perpetration of violence (table 8.3).

Characteristics of Productive and Perverse Social Institutions

The study also distinguished between productive and perverse institutions. Productive institutions aim to provide benefits to

Table 8.2 Importance of social institutions by type (*total number of institutions*)

Type of institution	Concepción, Guatemala City	Nuevo Horizonte, Guatemala City	La Merced, Guatemala City	San Jorge, Chinautla	Sacuma, Huehuetenango	Limoncito, San Marcos	El Carmen, Santa Lucía Cotzumalguapa	Villa Real, Esquipulas	Gucumatz, Santa Cruz del Quiché	Total
Membership Organizations										
Religious groups	7	15	13	20	8	9	15	13	5	105 (49.3)
Neighborhood committees	8	8	13	0	1	2	3	10	2	47 (22.1)
Youth, sports, and recreational organizations	8	8	5	0	3	0	0	0	1	25 (11.7)
Women's and childcare organizations	0	11	6	0	0	0	0	0	2	19 (8.9)
Violence-related groups	0	2	3	4	1	2	0	2	0	14 (6.6)
Organizations for the elderly	0	0	0	0	0	0	0	0	3	3 (1.4)
Subtotal	23	44	40	24	13	13	18	25	13	213
Service Delivery Organizations										
Social service organizations	7	27	30	14	18	18	31	1	36	182 (32)
NGOs	7	28	19	8	1	2	7	6	48	126 (22.1)
State/government organizations	2	0	4	6	5	6	14	7	49	93 (16.3)

State, security/justice institutions	0	6	11	0	7	3	18	6	20	71 (12.5)
Productive service organizations	1	2	0	1	3	11	10	4	23	59 (10.4)
Drug/alcohol rehabilitation centers	2	4	0	5	4	2	9	9	3	38 (6.7)
Private sector organizations	0	0	0	0	4	0	0	0	0	4 (0.7)
Subtotal	19	67	64	34	42	42	89	35	179	569
Total	**42**	**111**	**104**	**58**	**55**	**55**	**107**	**58**	**192**	**782**

Note: The category of religious groups refers to churches and prayer groups only; religious organizations that provide social services are included in the appropriate service delivery category.

Source: 126 institutional listings, Venn diagrams, and institutional preference matrixes from focus groups.

119

Table 8.3 Evaluation of trust in social institutions
(percent of respondents)

Type of Institution	High level of trust	Low level of trust
Membership organizations		
Neighborhood committees	68	33
Women's and child care organizations	76	23
Groups for the elderly	100	0
Youth, sports, and recreational organizations	82	18
Violence-related groups	0	100
Religious groups	79	21
Subtotal	68	32
Service delivery organizations		
Social service organizations	76	24
Drug/alcohol rehabilitation centers	81	19
State/government organizations	60	40
State, security/justice institutions	39	61
NGOs	66	34
Productive service organizations	49	51
Subtotal	64	36
Total	**65**	**35**

Note: A total of 558 evaluations of those in social institutions were undertaken through institutional mapping exercises in which "+" and "–" were put next to institutions to denote whether or not people trusted them. These identified 121 membership organizations and 437 service delivery organizations.
Source: 126 institutional listings, institutional mapping/Venn diagrams, and institutional preference matrixes from focus groups.

improve the well-being of the community. Perverse institutions benefit their members but are usually detrimental to the community or society at large (see Rubio 1997).

Most organizations identified in the nine communities were productive and linked to the state, NGOs, and the church. Perverse institutions were much less frequently mentioned and referred primarily to *maras*, drug dealers, or brothels and *cantinas*. A male community leader in Concepción, Guatemala City, identified four "illicit" groups in the *colonia* as two families who sold drugs, a man who organized adoption of babies for money, groups of *maras*, and a "runner" (*coyote*) who smuggled people across the U.S./Mexican border.

Maras were the most commonly identified perverse group. In Sacuma, Huehuetenango, two groups were identified as negative or harmful institutions (Figure 8.1). A focus group of mothers distinguished between one group of *maras* from within the community and another from outside. The latter comprised people who had come to Huehuetenango en route to crossing the Mexican border on their way to the United States. Unable to cross, many returned to the Guatemalan border towns, settling temporarily before trying again. The focus group noted that most of the *maras* from outside the community were Salvadorans (identified through their distinctive accent). In Sacuma, Huehuetenango, and Villa Real, Esquipulas, both border towns, Salvadorans and Hondurans formed *maras* when unable to cross the U.S./Mexican border.

Figure 8.1 Institutional mapping of Sacuma, Huehuetenango (drawn by a group of 10 mothers)

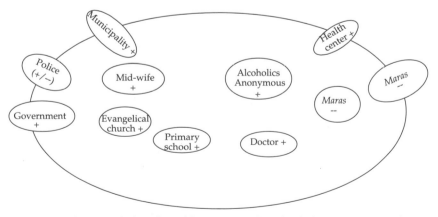

Note: Large circle denotes the boundary of the community. Size of circle denotes importance of institution; + and – denote whether trusted or not.

Lack of Institutional Diversity

Despite over 300 institutions identified in the nine communities, most *colonias* lacked institutional diversity. The majority of the institutions were service delivery organizations, with church groups the only membership organizations consistently present. With the exception of Gucumatz, Santa Cruz del Quiché, and some of the Guatemala City communities, community members often had problems pinpointing organizations. Those most commonly identified were schools, health centers, churches, the mayor or municipality, the police, one or two NGOs, and Alcoholics Anonymous. ·

A carpenter from Villa Real, Esquipulas, for instance, identified only four organizations within his community—the *cantina*, Alcoholics Anonymous, the evangelical churches, and a neighborhood support committee—with a further three located outside (figure 8.2). The three external organizations—the police, the

Figure 8.2 Institutional mapping of Villa Real, Esquipulas (prepared by a 39-year-old male carpenter)

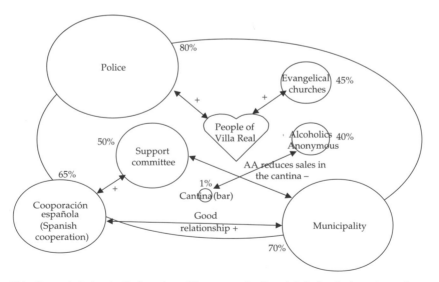

Notes: Large circle denotes the boundary of the community. Size of circle denotes importance of institution. Arrow denote relationships between institutions. Percentages denote the level of trust, with a high percentage denoting high level of trust.

Cooporación Española (Spanish Cooperation, the Spanish bilateral donor agency), and the municipality—were all perceived as more important than organizations within the community.

Hierarchical Institutions and the Role of International Agencies

Most institutions identified were hierarchical service delivery organizations. Community members recognized few grassroots-level organizations that were horizontal in structure. In Villa Real, Esquipulas, for instance, the police were the most trusted institution in the community, followed by the municipality and Cooporación Española (figure 8 ?) Although none of these had a physical presence in the community, they inspired greater trust than those located within the community. The impetus to establish an improvement committee came from the Cooporación Española through a municipal social worker. Community members were encouraged to address the canalization of an adjacent river, one of the main problems affecting them.

In Concepción, Guatemala City, three international organizations—Medicine Without Borders (Medecins sans Frontieres), the Norwegian church, and World Vision—played an important role in the community's development, especially during crucial phases of securing a water supply, and buying and legalizing plots of land (figure 8.3). Another focus group (comprising an elderly man and a young woman) identified five different organizations that had played an important role. In addition to the Norwegian church (active between 1986 and 1993) and World Vision, Care International assisted the municipality in the provision of drainage between 1986 and 1987, and Medicine Without Borders and UNICEF provided the first drinking water supply in 1994. A Guatemalan NGO involved in youth training programs has taken over the work of the Norwegian church. Local politicians had also played a role in the community, through the former President, Alvaro Arzú, when he was mayor of Guatemala City, and later when he was a presidential candidate. However, focus groups were disillusioned with the failed promises of Guatemalan politi-

Figure 8.3   Institutional mapping of Concepción, Guatemala City (prepared by a group of six adult men)

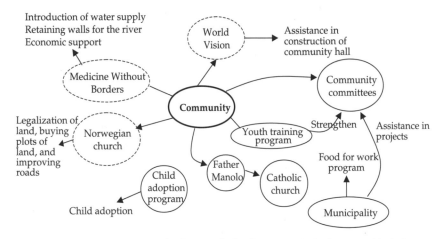

Note: Dotted circles are institutions that have worked in the community in the past and had a large impact.

cians and considered international organizations more trustworthy, because they were presumably not interested in vote buying.

This orientation toward foreign organizations reinforced paternalism within the organizational culture of communities. Although as in Villa Real, Esquipulas, some external agencies created local improvement committees, in other places, their presence discouraged grassroots organizing. In San Jorge, Chinautla, for example, one woman, said that: "The people in San Jorge want everything to fall from the sky," referring to their inability to organize themselves. Similarly, in Gucumatz, Santa Cruz del Quiché, the plethora of NGOs that arrived during the civil war has affected the nature of community organizing. One man noted how people have become accustomed to being given everything, rather than lobbying and organizing for themselves. He noted: "Before, everything was given away and the people grew accustomed to it; now nobody collaborates unless they are given something in exchange; now there is no community participation."

The Nature of Weak Community Social Capital

One reason for the orientation toward foreign, external, hierarchical organizations related to high levels of mistrust or, in other words, weak intracommunity cognitive social capital.

In all communities weak social capital ranged from outright violent conflict among neighbors to attitudes of people "keeping themselves to themselves." In Villa Real, Esquipulas, one woman commented about the relationship among neighbors: "We live like cats and dogs." Fights over access to land and legal tenure were a perennial source of conflict. In La Merced, Guatemala City, this related to the division, distribution, and legalization of plots of land through an urbanization program.[3] One woman, for example, noted that because of legal land tenure arguments, her house was set on fire and she and her family nearly burned. She was threatened with lynching for confronting some community leaders.

In Limoncito, San Marcos, violence occurred among community members fighting over market stalls located within the community. Although the mayor had tried to encourage market sellers to move to a new market area nearer the center of the town, people wanted to stay in the original area. Two men who had stalls in the market showed how arguments over space often erupted in street fights (figure 8.4).

Quality and access to water was another source of physical and verbal conflict among neighbors. Widespread contamination of water caused diseases (especially of the digestive tract), and disruptions in access to water often resulted in fights. When water supplies were cut off for long periods of time, people stole water from others who had it stored—or accused them of stealing it. These water-related problems were especially marked in Gucumatz, Santa Cruz del Quiché; and Limoncito, San Marcos. In Santa Cruz del Quiché, the municipality was set on fire as a protest about water shortages in the town.

While both men and women participated in these fights, some broke out between women. These were mainly verbal, although some resulted in physical violence. Conflicts included arguments over men or children, usually in the form of gossip. These often

Figure 8.4   Causal impact diagram of fights over market stalls in Limoncito, San Marcos (prepared by two adult men aged 23 and 32)

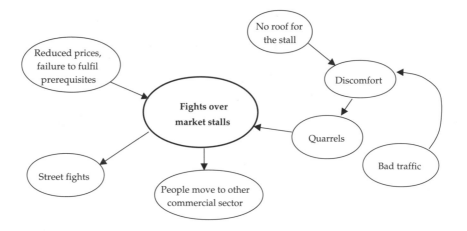

started among schoolchildren. In Sacuma, Huehuetenango, for instance, a group of girls from the local primary school identified that reasons for fights among girls ranged from jealousy to envy relating to men and beauty (figure 8.5).

Lack of cohesion also manifested itself in the nature of people's spatial awareness within the community. They were often unwilling to discuss the *colonia* as a whole, instead being prepared to talk about their block, street, or alley. This was associated with resistance to engage in the lives of neighbors. In Limoncito, San Marcos, an elderly woman stated that: "No one gets involved in the lives of others," while another woman in the same *colonia* said, "Everyone lives their own lives." People rarely went out in the evenings, locking themselves in their homes for the night between 6 and 8 o'clock in the evening.

This obviously undermined people's willingness to participate in community activities. In La Merced, Guatemala City, an adult woman said that no one participated in any communal activities because of resulting conflict and gossip. She stated, "We don't like to participate because there are neighbors who talk about us, and we don't want to get involved in problems because people will talk about us."

Figure 8.5 Causal impact diagram of fights among girl students in Sacuma, Huehuetenango (prepared by a group of 11 girls in primary school)

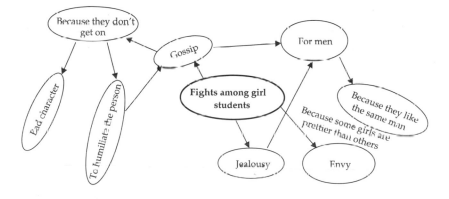

Many focus groups cited accusations of corruption against neighborhood committees. In Concepción, Guatemala City, a woman treasurer of the neighborhood improvement committee admitted that, even among the members of the board, there was little communication or trust. In Gucumatz, Santa Cruz del Quiché, one man pointed out that weak leadership was because community leaders had either been killed or had disappeared in the 1980s. As a result, people were still afraid to participate in activities that could potentially cause reprisals.

The Causes of Weak Community Social Capital

As noted in chapter 3 lack of cohesion in all the communities related directly, or indirectly, to Guatemala's post-conflict status, rebuilding itself after a civil war. Throughout the country the violence and brutality of the political conflict have destroyed trust and the social fabric of communities.[4] Even in the research communities that had not directly experienced the political violence of the war, regardless of ethnicity, an aura of mistrust prevailed.

Undermining social capital was the culture of silence that affected all the communities, but it was most pronounced in the predominantly indigenous community of Gucumatz, Santa Cruz del Quiché, which suffered considerably during the political conflict. One man from this community recalled the 1980s when the conflict was most severe: "If someone talked, he was a dead man; for this reason, people kept silent." Another remembered how a gathering of two or more people was regarded as subversive and could lead to murder, recounting that they couldn't even hold a funeral without fear of being killed themselves. This reluctance to speak has continued today, with another man in the same community noting, "Today no one takes responsibility for anything; only dead men...the survivors live in silence." Many people from Gucumatz pointed out that despite the Peace Accords they were still afraid of repression. While *ladinos* expressed such views, indigenous people in focus groups were most likely to comment on the implications of political conflict.

Underlying weak community social capital was fear, linked to potential or actual violence. Although people still feared the return of political violence, in many cases this was now manifested in fear of delinquency, robbery, and *maras* resulting from insufficient state security force protection. A mother and daughter from La Merced, Guatemala City, showed how fear of theft and rape (figure 8.6) limited their mobility, with the gossip about the types of crimes committed in the *colonia* underlying much of this.

As noted in an earlier chapter, people complained of the stigma associated with their *colonias*. In Concepción, Guatemala City, for instance, residents explained that people from outside refused to come into their *colonia* because they were afraid of violence, and that shops wouldn't give them credit when they heard where they lived.

Indigenous people more commonly mentioned fear than did *ladinos* (the mother and daughter in figure 8.6, for example, were indigenous). Indigenous focus groups noted that the atrocities of the civil war had contributed to the culture of silence and the generation of fear in their communities. One man in Gucumatz noted: "How do I know you are a good person ... you think I'm stupid, that's what they did in the past...when you turned round they changed their shirt/tune." However, many also suggested that increasing economic and social violence since the signing of the Peace Accords generated a different form of fear. Because of a

Figure 8.6 Causal impact diagram of fear in La Merced, Guatemala City (identified by a mother aged 38 and daughter aged 16, who worked in a tortilla-making enterprise)

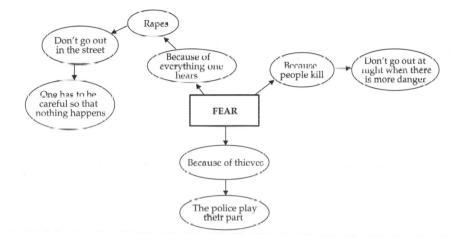

tradition of persecution and fear among indigenous groups, they were the most likely to express these sentiments.

The Role of Churches

In all the communities, churches were among the most prevalent and important membership organizations. Indeed, in San Jorge, Chinautla, churches were the only membership organizations identified besides the *maras*. These included Roman Catholic and evangelical churches (especially the Church of Nazarene, the Church of God, the Church of God is Love, Pentecostals, and Jehovah's Witnesses), with evangelical churches the most widespread in communities.[5] All the *colonias* had at least two or three evangelical meeting houses as well as many private evangelical primary and secondary schools. According to two shoemakers in Limoncito, San Marcos, for example, the evangelical church dominated community institutions in terms of the number of actual churches and church-run primary and secondary schools (figure 8.7). Indeed, as in Limoncito, San Marcos in many communities the most commonly identified institutions were churches, *cantinas*, brothels, and Alcoholics Anonymous (figure 8.7).

Despite their preponderance, evangelical churches were not always positively evaluated, and frequently criticized for creating divisions within communities (although perceptions differed between Catholics and evangelicals). In Villa Real, Esquipulas, there was marked tension between Catholics and evangelicals. One Catholic woman said that when her neighbors became evangelicals they stopped talking to her. Another woman who knew many men had joined the church while continuing to beat their wives, complained of the evangelical church's hypocrisy. More pragmatically, two young women from El Carmen, Santa Lucía Cotzumalguapa, noted that the Catholic church was better because it organized trips to Esquipulas—while the evangelical churches only organized fasts.[6] Generally the Catholic churches were perceived to be less controversial and viewed more favorably. However, there were variations; in San Jorge, Chinautla,

Figure 8.7 Institutional mapping of Limoncito, San Marcos (prepared by two shoemakers aged 28 and 50)

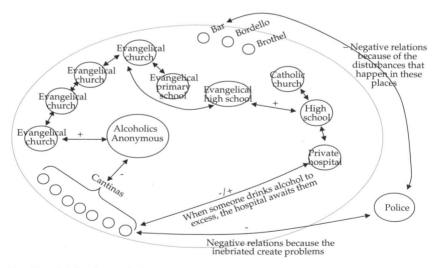

Note: Size of circles denotes the importance of the institution to the community. +/− denotes the perception of positive or negative for the community.

divisionism between the two churches was blamed on the Catholic priest who was held in very low regard, yet in Concepción, Guatemala City, the local priest was widely respected. Overall, within communities that already suffered from lack of solidarity, the evangelical churches created even more tensions and mistrust.

Cofradías[7] were an additional religious and political institution, identified in communities with predominantly indigenous populations—such as Gucumatz, Santa Cruz del Quiché; San Jorge, Chinautla; and to a lesser extent in El Carmen, Santa Lucía Cotzumalguapa. Originally a lay brotherhood within the Catholic church, Mayan groups transformed cofradías into a political organization responsible for maintaining Mayan customs and beliefs. Comprising male elders, the cofradías took care of the patron saint. However, because of the persecution of associations related with Mayan identity, cofradías were not that widespread. Nevertheless, in Gucumatz they were viewed as important institutions and as ways to strengthen the social fabric of the indigenous community. One man viewed their meetings as very successful, noting, "Around 80 families come to the cofradía and we share nine days of prayer and four days of marimba, alcohol, and food." However, in San Jorge, Chinautla, the cofradía was viewed with less enthusiasm; while one community leader stated that their meetings were just an excuse to drink, another said that they existed as a symbol rather than doing anything very useful for the community.

Perceptions of the Police

Confidence in the state security and justice systems was very low, with over 60 percent of people mistrusting them. However, attitudes varied, depending on whether the community was served by the reformed police force—the National Civil Police (Policía Nacional Civil, PNC)—or the "former" force—the National Police (Policía Nacional, PN).[8] As a result of police reform involving retraining police officers and appointing new recruits, the new PNC was held in much higher regard than its predecessor (see also chapter 7 on maras, robbers, and delinquents).

In stark contrast, the PN was universally condemned. A 50-year-old woman in Limoncito, San Marcos, commented that the PN was worse than the delinquents and robbers they were supposed to be catching. They drunkenly traversed the community firing their guns indiscriminately so that people had to hide. She concluded that it was the "old police force" that destroyed the community. Contempt for the PN led to violent protest in El Carmen, Santa Lucía Cotzumalguapa. One focus group recalled how the police station was burnt down twice; first in 1990 because the police did nothing about a North American woman accused of stealing children to take to the United States for adoption; second, in 1991, in protest that the police were not bringing delinquents to justice.

In most of the study communities police reform and the replacement of the PN by the PNC had been introduced. While perceptions of the "new police" were not always favorable, they were more positive than those of their predecessors. For instance, in Nuevo Horizonte, Guatemala City, a woman working in a tortilla-making shop spoke of the PNC: "The police are good now that they're the civil force; they look after the community and when they're called they come and investigate." In the same community numerous people confirmed that they felt much safer now than before. In Villa Real, Esquipulas, people reported that the police made twice-daily "tours" of the *colonia* and distributed their phone number for emergency needs (figure 8.8). An elderly woman also noted that they had intervened in domestic disputes a number of times, something that the "old police" (PN) would never have done.

In communities such as Nuevo Horizonte and La Merced, Guatemala City, and Villa Real, Esquipulas, where the PNC were generally welcomed, many noted that violence had declined since the PNC arrived. The Deputy Chief of the Police Station in La Merced, Guatemala City, noted that three types of violence he considered as most significant in the community—delinquency, *maras,* and intrafamily violence—had all declined since the PNC arrived. He suggested that delinquency had decreased 40 percent, and that violence in general had declined by 60 percent. He considered that this had been achieved through greater vigilance

Figure 8.8   Perceptions of the police in Villa Real, Esquipulas
(prepared by one elderly man and one elderly woman)

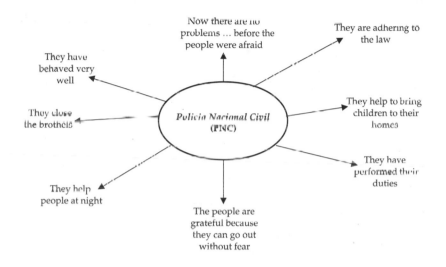

on their part through patrols, as well as paying more attention
to community members' complaints.

In Villa Real, Esquipulas, where community members reported similar patterns, a focus group discussed how violence
levels had changed over time (figure 8.9). In 1994, the *colonia* was
dominated by armed groups, described by some as paramilitaries
organized by the military and police force to deal with delinquency. The height of the assassinations came in 1996, due to
high levels of "social cleansing," with a marked decline after the
death of Tito (who was responsible for the social cleansing—see
box 8.1) and the arrival of the PNC in 1999.

Despite such favorable perceptions of the PNC, many still
mistrusted them and reported police corruption everywhere. This
was most marked in Gucumatz, Santa Cruz del Quiché, especially among Mayan-dominated focus groups. One focus group
of young indigenous people maintained that the police were only
interested in causing damage in the community, creating rather
than solving problems: "The police are really bad because they
are not helping the community and they are interested only in

Figure 8.9   Timeline of changes in violence in Villa Real, Esquipulas, 1990–99 (drawn by two young women aged 22 and 23)

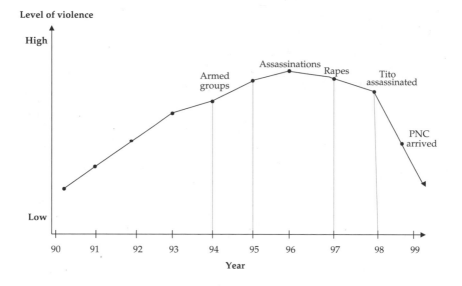

causing damage because they don't practice justice." In El Carmen, Santa Lucía Cotzumalguapa, a Mayan couple noted that the police took bribes of 3,000 *quetzales* ($429) to release prisoners, and that there was no justice in the town. A *ladino* man in Concepción, Guatemala City, commented that there was no police support in the community because they did nothing to help the population: "I have never gone to the police because one just becomes another name on the list that is put into the archives."

Perceptions of Justice and Lynching

All communities noted the lack of justice and the inefficiency of the judicial system on the part of the police and other state actors, including the military. Indeed, in Gucumatz, Santa Cruz del Quiché, one group of three men and one woman considered police inefficiency as a form of violence, complaining of the "slowness of justice—because when a thief is captured he is released immediately." Even the mayor in Esquipulas identified lack of

justice as one of the major problems affecting the town. He reported as the cause of this the "lack of application of justice by
the judges," "lack of police agents," and "fear of police agents."
The outcome of the lack of justice had been massacres and fights,
especially revenge killings and people taking justice into their
own hands.

Extrajudicial killings or lynchings had increased since the
signing of the Peace Accords (PNUD 1998:147). Lynching usually involved injuring or killing someone accused of committing
a crime, often dousing the target with petrol and setting them
alight.[9] Lynching was directly related to impunity and lack of
faith in the formal justice system (Ferrigno 1998). Although lynching was not common in the communities, most had some experience of the phenomenon. In La Merced, Guatemala City, for
example, numerous focus groups recalled the recent lynching of
three men who had been accused of gang-raping a young girl.
Community members had pursued and murdered the men in
their frustration that the police and judicial system had done
nothing about it. A group of two female and three male municipal employees in Santa Cruz del Quiché identified lynching as a
major problem in the town, commenting that the inefficacy of
the police meant this was the only way that people felt they could
secure justice. They felt pessimistic about the future, stating that
lynching would continue until the authorities implemented a just
justice system. In Villa Real, Esquipulas, in particular, there was
a long history of systematic lynching through social cleansing
(*limpieza social*) (box 8.1).

The Reconstruction of Productive Social Institutions and Women-Dominated Organizations

Although women's organizations and childcare groups were
only identified in three of the research communities—Nuevo
Horizonte and La Merced, Guatemala City; and Gucumatz, Santa
Cruz del Quiché—they played an important role in these communities. In La Merced, for example, there were six of these organizations, outnumbered only by churches and neighborhood
committees. One of these women's organizations, UPAVIM, pro-

Box 8.1 Social cleansing in Villa Real, Esquipulas: The case of Tito

In Villa Real, Esquipulas, many community members discussed how social cleansing had affected their *colonia* in the past. It began in 1995 with the arrival of a person called Tito, who previously had been a member of the army, forming part of a military network responsible for recruiting young men to the army in the 1980s. Tito had received military training, including *"kaibil"* that taught extremely violent counterinsurgency strategies. According to those who knew him, training courses such as these made Tito insane, turning him into a killer.

Tito, together with some companions, was in charge of killing all the "undesirables" and delinquents in the community. He was ordered to carry out this task by the "highly corrupt authorities in Esquipulas." When the bodies began to appear, an atmosphere of terror engulfed the *colonia*. Yet, at the same time, levels of delinquency declined considerably. While, on the one hand, Tito was considered a hero because most people approved of the extra-judicial murders, on the other hand, people were afraid of him.

Fear of him increased when he began to kill people who had nothing to do with delinquency. For instance, he began to work as a paid assassin conducting revenge assassinations. In addition, he killed former companions because they had witnessed the murders. Over time, people hated rather than feared him. On January 7, 1998, some unknown men from outside the *colonia* shot him dead in the back. After his death, many people felt that levels of violence had decreased in the community.

Source: Various focus group discussions, Villa Real, Esquipulas.

---

vided a wide range of services including income-generating activities, childcare, health care, and training courses. For those involved, UPAVIM was referred to as a "lifeline," while others, on the waiting list to join and without access to the center, discussed it in a disparaging way. Overall, though, UPAVIM and other women's organizations strengthen and foster social capital. One woman in La Merced, for instance, identified a *crèche*, another women's training center, and Doña Elsa who was perceived as an institution herself as well as UPAVIM (figure 8.10).

Figure 8.10 Institutional mapping of La Merced, Guatemala City (drawn by an adult woman)

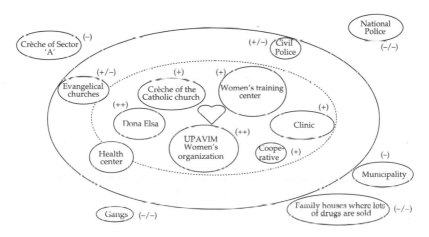

Note: (++) = very positive; (+) – positive; (+/–) = regular; (–) = negative; (–/–) = very negative.

This chapter describes the impact of different types of violence on social organizations, both informal and formal, within communities, with particular reference to the impact of violence on social capital. Within the limitations of local community-based institutions highlighted here, the following chapter concludes by documenting community perceptions of strategies and solutions to violence in Guatemala.

Notes

1. Information on individual organizational membership was not gathered since the participatory urban appraisal methodology does not use questionnaire surveys (see for example, Groothaert 1999; Narayan 1997). However, a particular advantage of participatory appraisal is its ability to identify illegal or criminal violence-related groups in a context of anonymity.

2. Although organizations for the elderly were evaluated at 100 percent, this referred only to one organization.

3. This program, PROUME (*Proyecto de Urbanización Mesquital*) is funded by the World Bank and implemented through UNICEF.

4. See, for example, ODHAG (1999).

5. This reflects wider patterns in Guatemala as a whole. Evangelical churches began to flourish in the early 1980s, encouraged by the evangelical General Ríos Montt who became president in 1982. He opened Guatemala's doors to many U.S.-based evangelical churches (O'Kane 1999).

6. Esquipulas is a city of religious pilgrimage where people go to visit the *Cristo Negro* (Black Christ) who they believe performs miracles.

7. *Cofradias* are historically recognized institutional structures among indigenous groups of political and social importance.

8. Reform of the police force was part of the Peace Accords of 1996. More specifically, this included "The Agreement on the Strengthening of Civilian Power and the Role of the Armed Forces in a Democratic Society" through which the government agreed to form a new civilian police force.

9. MINUGUA notes that 67 percent of those lynched had committed crimes against property. In most cases, they occurred when investigation into the offense or crime was not conducted, and people felt moved to punish the accused themselves. In turn, lynchings were rarely investigated (MINUGUA 1998b:33).

9

Community Perceptions
of Solutions to Violence

The final chapter documents community perceptions of solutions to violence in the communities. A salient issue is
how community members identified solutions to violence
as linked with social capital and human capital. Interventions
designed to reduce political violence were confined to solutions
relating to human capital. The overall failure to acknowledge the
capacity of physical capital to resolve violence suggests that community members did not identify solutions to economic, social,
and political violence as having a direct relationship with wider
structural issues. Instead, they tended to think in the short term,
as reflected in discussion groups relating to both coping strategies and solutions.

Coping Strategies to Deal with Violence

Strategies for coping with violence can be divided into four categories: avoidance, confrontation, conciliation, and other strategies (Moser 1996, 1998) (table 9.1).

Most people reported adopting *avoidance mechanisms* that included changing their mobility patterns and "ignoring the situation." Widespread fear of retribution, of powerlessness, and of
exacerbating the situation induced these responses. Maintaining
silence was particularly notable with regard to economic crimes,

Table 9.1   Strategies for coping with violence
(*percent of total*)

Type of coping strategy	Frequency	Percentage
Avoidance strategies		
Avoid 'bad company/friends'	8	4
Avoid those involved in violence related activities	4	2
Silence/ignore situation	17	9
Change spatial mobility patterns	21	11
Change mobility patterns temporally— don't go out at night	19	10
Scream	4	2
Leave your husband	2	1
Flee	7	4
Change habits of dress (in the case of rape) and be a good wife (in the case of intrafamily violence)	2	1
Don't carry valuables	2	1
Leave *barrio*	5	3
Lock houses/put bars on windows	8	4
Confrontation strategies		
Confrontation	4	2
Carry weapons	4	2
Use violence	6	3
Conciliation strategies		
Develop relations with those involved in violence	2	1
Turn to religion/pray for those involved	8	4
Others		
Report to human rights institutions	2	1
Report to the judge or other institutions	10	5
Report to family members, neighbors or teachers	21	11
Report to police	27	15
Submit, cry, abort pregnancy (in the case of rape)	3	4
Total	**187**	**100**

Note: The types of violence-related problems include drugs, insecurity, intrafamily violence, perverse social institutions, rape, robbery, murder, and fights in the street. *Source*: 176 focus group listings.

such as robbery and gang violence. However, as in Concepción, Guatemala City, participants noted that silence was also a strategy used in the case of rape (see chapter 3). In San Jorge, Chinautla, silence was also maintained in the case of intrafamily violence (see chapter 4). One woman from San Jorge stated, "Often we just stay silent, do nothing, when there's violence in the family."

The other predominant avoidance strategy entailed changing mobility patterns within communities, both temporally and permanently. Many people avoided places where gangs and drug addicts congregated, changing their walking routes to avoid such places, and at night, seeking areas with streetlights. In the case of Sacuma, Huehuetenango, this strategy was women's response to rape. Community members also reported how they severely restricted their activities after dark, locking themselves in their houses from as early as 6 o'clock, but in most cases after 9 o'clock when the incidence of violence dramatically increased. Women were most likely to report these responses, although both men and women explained how they avoided going out alone. Participants from La Merced and Concepción, Guatemala City, spelt out that they tried to ensure their children stayed in at night to keep them away from gangs and drugs. A male adult from Concepción stated: "We have to keep our children entertained and teach them skills so that they don't get involved in gangs."

Other strategies included avoiding perpetrators of crime and violence-related activities. Young people kept away from people they feared would lead them astray, such as drug dealers and friends involved in gangs, drug taking, or delinquency. Parents from Nuevo Horizonte, Guatemala City, described how they tried to keep their children busy on weekends to reduce the likelihood that they would be in contact with drugs. Other people described the way they fled from violent situations as a means of coping—particularly with gang- and drug-related violence, whether as witnesses or victims. Participants, especially women, also stressed that they do not wear jewelry, to avoid robbery. A similar strategy was described by a young woman from El Carmen, Santa Lucía Cotzumalguapa: "You have to take care of yourself to deal with rape and one way is by dressing decently and not wearing short skirts."

Confrontation and conciliation strategies were far less common, because of fear of violent repercussions. A group of two men and one woman from Concepción, Guatemala City, reported carrying firearms or other weapons with which they could defend themselves against robberies and assaults. A similar strategy was reported by a focus group of four youths in San Jorge, Chinautla, who described how they would defend themselves against gangs by using arms. Women in Nuevo Horizonte, Guatemala City, noted self-defense as a form of response to rape, stating that it was important to "bite or scream in response to rape."

Although most people avoided perpetrators, on a few occasions, some young people reported getting to know those involved in crime as a means of protecting themselves. The predominant conciliation strategy, however, involved religion. Participants prayed both for those involved in crime and for their victims, and they joined the evangelical church, in particular, as a means of responding to violent circumstances. This tendency was particularly notable in Gucumatz, Santa Cruz del Quiché, where an adult woman stated that "religious sects are important for solving violence" and that "thieves are scared of God."

Other mechanisms for dealing with violence involved reporting conflicts or violent events to the authorities. This was particularly apparent in the case of robbery or gang-related crime. A man from Sacuma, Huehuetenango, identified that when a violent event took place, "We go to a human rights organization that will investigate the crime or sometimes to the police that follow up the report through the public ministry." Levels of reporting intrafamily violence and rape were especially high and, in the case of rape, included informing both doctors and the local judge. In Gucumatz, Santa Cruz del Quiché, and La Merced, Guatemala City, strategies to deal with intrafamily violence also included making complaints to human rights institutions. Schoolteachers often instructed children and young people about the dangers of violence. In other instances, participants reported violent activities to the local judge. In some cases of sexual abuse and intrafamily violence, however, fear caused people to cope with their problems alone, without reporting them.

Interventions to Reduce Violence

Participants combined both short-term strategies and longer-term interventions to deal with the violent conditions in their communities. More than half the solutions were associated with strengthening or building social capital (see tables 9.2 and 9.3). Within this category, the promotion of dialogue and unity (cognitive social capital) and the formation of organizations (structural social capital) within communities were the most important recurrent interventions. For example, a young woman from Concepción, Guatemala City, stated that "we need to communicate well and advise each other, and we have to treat our children well to create trust in the community."

Figure 9.1 Interventions for reducing violence in Villa Real, Esquipulas (identified by an adult woman aged 38)

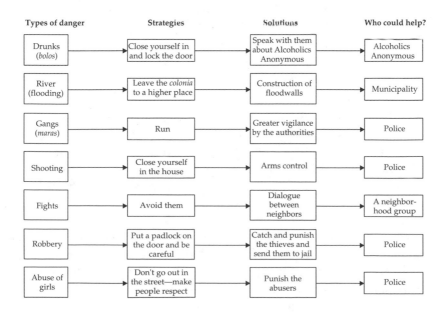

Table 9.2   Summary of interventions to reduce violence
(*percent*)

Intervention	Percent of Total
Increase social capital	
Productive social capital	35
Perverse social capital	23
Increase human capital	31
Increase physical capital	11
Total	**100**

In figure 9.1 a woman from Villa Real, Esquipulas, showed the way in which strategies and solutions to reduce violence needed to be combined. The different interventions identified brought together strengthening social capital (dialogue between people and community mobilization), human capital (especially talks concerning alcoholism), and physical capital (the construction of floodwalls and increased security in the home). This clearly showed the necessity for diverse strategies and solutions to simultaneously confront the different types of violence.

Increasing Social Capital

Social capital interventions were the most important type of intervention in all communities. *Productive social capital* interventions outnumbered *perverse social capital* interventions in seven out of the nine communities. However, in total, perverse social capital constituted over 40 percent of social capital interventions.

The most significant productive solutions were aimed at the generation of trust, family values, and unity, and the creation, reactivation, or strengthening of community organizations. These interventions addressed the building of both cognitive and structural social capital. In many cases, the latter consisted of fostering community-wide participation in local development committees and neighborhood watch–schemes. A woman from Nuevo Horizonte, Guatemala City, explained that "we have to organize ourselves and raise awareness in the community" in order to reduce violence. Similarly, a young woman in Villa Real, Esquipulas, explained the need "to generate dialogue and form a group of neighbors that will take care of the community." Some communities, including Gucumatz, Santa Cruz del Quiché, emphasized the importance of religion, in particular of evangelical Protestantism, in generating trust and social capital.

Of the 40 percent of social capital interventions involving repressive and potentially violent activities, the most widely recurrent negative solution concerned strengthening the presence of the state and the military. For example, an adult male from Sacuma, Huehuetenango, stated that, "We need more control by the authorities and they need to practice better justice in the communities." Other measures emphasized the need for offenders to serve long prison sentences and for the authorities to implement measures that would ensure they did not escape.

Social cleansing was also prioritized as a means to address violence. This included killing drug addicts, thieves, prostitutes, and delinquents, and the castration of rapists. For example, a focus group of women from El Carmen, Santa Lucía Cotzumalguapa, stated that rapists should be shot and killed (that is, lynched) (figure 9.2). However, such measures were combined with less repressive interventions such as prison sentences for offenders and strategies for taking care of oneself, such as keeping doors locked in the home. In contrast to demands for "more authority," social cleansing was a very different repressive social capital solution. This was a direct response to community members' perceptions concerning the absence and ineffectiveness of state institutions and the judicial system.

Perverse solutions were most often recommended in Sacuma, Huehuetenango, followed closely by recommendations for repressive interventions in Villa Real, Esquipulas, and San Jorge, Chinautla. There was also an important gender dimension in the suggested perverse social capital interventions. Men were more likely to likely to favor such perverse solutions, although in some contexts women too supported such measures, most notably in the case of rape. This was particularly marked in the community of El Carmen, Santa Lucía Cotzumalguapa (figure 9.2).

Figure 9.2   Intervention for reducing rape in El Carmen, Santa Lucía Cotzumalguapa (identified by 38 young women aged 12–17)

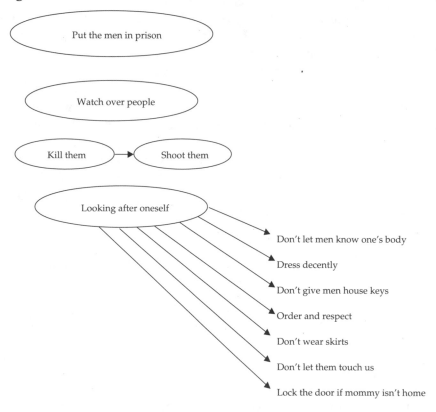

In San Jorge, Chinautla, a focus group of three young men emphasized the importance of combined strategies to deal with rape (figure 9.3). In illustrating their male perceptions of tackling the problem, they advocated avoidance mechanisms (not going out at night or not going to lonely places) together with solutions to strengthen social capital. This included both generating productive social capital by more police presence in the community, and repressive social capital interventions such as increased military presence in the community. Finally, they also included interventions to strengthen physical capital (the installation of streetlights and security in unlit places) (figure 9.3).

Figure 9.3 Interventions for reducing rape in San Jorge, Chinaulta (identified by three young men aged 14–17)

Increasing Human Capital

Human capital solutions represented almost one-third of the total interventions identified by community members, among which drug and alcohol rehabilitation and programs focusing on the young were the most commonly cited solutions. An indigenous teacher from San Jorge, Chinautla, for example, stated that "We need educational and rehabilitation programs in our community to reduce alcoholism, but these are hard to organize because people lack motivation." A group of eight young women from La Merced, Guatemala City, not only identified a number of different solutions, but also listed a diversity of social actors and institutions that "should do it" (box 9.1).

Box 9.1   Perceived solutions to drug addiction, in La Merced, Guatemala City (identified by eight young women aged 14-18)

Problem	Solution	Who should do it?	Expected changes
Drug addiction	Give advice to young people, children, and drug addicts	Adults Young people Those it has happened to Security forces	No robbery No drug addiction Tranquility Well-being
	Provide rehabilitation Friends	Government Parents	
	Strengthen communication between parents and children	Church Friends School	

Increasing Physical Capital

References to the increase of physical capital were rare, representing 10 percent of all proposed interventions. In almost all cases participants prioritized the need to generate employment as a means of addressing violence. For example, an adult male from Gucumatz, Santa Cruz del Quiché, explained how "It is necessary to create work and share it throughout society as a way of confronting violence." However, people also focused on the need for infrastructural development, most notably for streetlights in their communities (figure 9.3), and for the regulation of the sale of alcohol and firearms.

Violence Reduction Solutions and Ethnicity

No fixed patterns linked specific ethnic groups to particular solutions to violence in the research communities. Both positive and negative social capital solutions were chosen to confront diverse types of violence, regardless of ethnic group. Positive so-

Table 9.3 Interventions for reducing violence, by type of capital and community *(percent of total)*

Type of capital	Concepción, Guatemala City	Nuevo Horizonte, Guatemala City	La Merced, Guatemala City	Sacuma, Huehuetenango	Limoncito, San Marcos	El Carmen, Santa Lucía Cotzumalguapa	Villa Real, Esquipulas	Gucumatz, Santa Cruz del Quiché	San Jorge, Chinautla	Total
Physical capital solutions	**5**	**8**	**11**	**15**	**12**	**8**	**16**	**16**	**7**	**11**
Job creation	2.5	5	9	9	5	5	2	12	3	5
Infrastructure provision				1	7	3	2	2	3	1
Build more prisons		1								1
Household security (locks, bars)									2	1
Urban planning				1						1
Disarming offenders/ control of firearms	2.5	1								1
Poverty reduction				2			7			1
Prohibition of the sale of alcohol		1	2	2			5	2		1
Human capital solutions	**37**	**34**	**37**	**31**	**42**	**24**	**24**	**22**	**26**	**31**
Academic and vocational education and scholarships	10	5	9	1	5	6	5	6	11	7
Drug and alcohol rehabilitation	8	13	5	9	10	2	12	2	4	8
Talks on drugs, sex education, and violence for youth	8	10	5	10	4	6	2	6	2	7
Training, orientation, and therapy		2		4	2	5	3			3
Sports and recreation	3	2	2	2	10			5	2	3
Conflict resolution education	3	1			4					1
Family counseling	5	1	16	5	7	5	2	2	7	3

(Table continues on next page.)

Table 9.3 (*continued*)

Type of capital	Concepción, Guatemala City	Nuevo Horizonte, Guatemala City	La Merced, Guatemala City	Sacuma, Huehue-tenango	Limoncito, San Marcos	El Carmen, Santa Lucía Cotzumal-guapa	Villa Real, Esqui-pulas	Gucumatz, Santa Cruz del Quiché	San Jorge, Chi-nautla	Total
Social capital solutions	**58**	**58**	**52**	**54**	**46**	**68**	**60**	**62**	**67**	**58**
Productive social capital										
Promotion of family values	8	7.5	15	3	6	19	6	13	2	7
More governmental institutions	3							4		1
Formation of cognitive social capital (trust)	3	13	9	5	8	9	5	5	19	8
Formation of structural social capital (organizations)	5	15	2	4	6	2	5	3	3	5
Use of religious organizations			4	2	4	3	2	13	9	3
More human rights institutions		3				3				2
Greater police presence	5	7.5	9	6	12	8	13	2	9	7
Perverse social capital										
More discipline in families	3	1		2						3
Deport foreign gang leaders				2			4	3	7	2
Social cleansing	8	1		6		8	2		2	5
Military protection/stronger state presence	8	2	11	12	5	6	8	8	9	7
Catch criminals and longer prison sentences	15	8	2	12	5	10	15	11	7	8
Total	**100**	**100**	**100**	**100**	**100**	**100**	**100**	**100**	**100**	**100**

Source: 176 focus group listings.

150

cial capital solutions included the creation of structural social capital and cognitive social capital.

However, the increasingly frequent decision by *ladino* groups to make use of human rights organizations as a means of resolving conflicts and confronting violence has been a significant development. This was notable in several communities, with *ladinos* seeking to resolve rape, *mara* activity, and intrafamily violence in this way. Indigenous groups used human rights organizations in a similar way, but they also used them for problems of political violence, often related to discrimination. Thus human rights organizations, historically representative predominantly of the indigenous population for political abuses, are now broadening to include the *ladino* population and also to resolve cases of social and economic violence. This also indicates that, as patterns of violence themselves have changed, so have people's perceptions of what constitutes their human rights.

Constraints and Recommendations

Despite the signing of the Peace Accords urban poor communities perceived that violence still pervades their communities. Indeed in some cases they considered it worse in the post-conflict phase than during the civil war itself. The perceptions of the poor, therefore, can help policymakers in both government and civil society to formulate appropriate violence-reduction policies. Local communities identified three interrelated national-level constraints to solving the problem of violence:

- *Extensive fear and distrust.* The legacy of decades of civil war and armed conflict is an extreme level of fear, frequently manifested in a culture of silence. This has resulted in a lack of social cohesion within communities, mistrust even of neighbors and friends, and associated low levels of both structural and cognitive social capital.
- *Discrimination against and exclusion of the indigenous population.* Human rights violations and counterinsurgency policy particularly targeted at the indigenous population during the civil war, as well as continuing racial and cultural discrimination, results in the persistent exclusion of these groups

within Guatemalan society. This has exacerbated their levels of fear and social cohesion even in the post-conflict context.

- *Lack of trust or confidence in the police and judicial system.* The severe lack of confidence in the government's capacity to provide adequate police or judicial protection fosters development of alternative informal justice systems (including social cleansing such as lynching. Nevertheless, the new *Policia Nacional Civil* (PNC) is held in much higher regard than the former *Policia Nacional* (PN)—with associated lower levels of delinquency, robbery, and violence in communities served by the PNC.

Local-level recommendations for reducing violence can be summarized in terms of six priorities:

- *Rebuild trust in the police and judicial system.* Despite partial progress to address this issue through, for instance, the introduction of the PNC in some areas, fundamental measures are still needed to rebuild trust at the local level if informal justice and social cleansing are to be eliminated. This includes countrywide introduction of the PNC along with extensive interventions to build their capacity and reduce corruption in the police force. Fear and distrust on the part of the indigenous population will remain until human rights abuses and reconciliation issues are transparently addressed through the judicial system.
- *Attack the problem of alcoholism.* The high level of alcohol consumption was one of the most important concerns in all communities. A comprehensive strategy must include prevention through increased public awareness, as well as rehabilitation of alcoholics. Implementing such a solution requires collaboration among education, health, social welfare, and other sectors, as well as between the government and NGOs such as Alcoholics Anonymous that have long battled the problem.
- *Reduce society's tolerance for intrafamily violence.* All communities acknowledged the high levels of social violence within the home. Dealing with both physical and mental abuse requires a strategy that encompasses both prevention and rehabilitation and can be constructively linked to alcohol-abuse

prevention programs. Given the high levels of tolerance in Guatemala for intrafamily violence, a holistic approach, with extensive interagency, media, and NGO collaboration, may help to begin to meet the demand from communities to address this issue so that it includes the needs of women and children alike.

- *Prevent the spread of drug consumption.* To date drug consumption is more concentrated in the capital and has not yet reached epidemic proportions on a nationwide scale, yet it is a critical concern in most communities. While preventative programs are needed to control the increasing spread of drugs to towns outside the capital, larger urban areas also require rehabilitation programs. This requires collaboration across sectors in the government, as well as between the government and NGOs.
- *Transform* maras *from perverse to productive social organizations.* Given the growing preoccupation with *maras* in poor urban communities, and the distinctions among them—ranging from highly violent gangs to support structures for local youth—innovative inclusive programs could involve young people themselves in overcoming violence-related problems. Such interventions could include drug prevention, issues of self-esteem, as well as skills-training to access local employment opportunities. To dissolve the highly violent gangs in larger urban areas may require both punitive and rehabilitation initiatives.
- *Develop mechanisms to build sustainable community-based membership organizations.* Rebuilding the fabric of local communities and their social organizations, with trust and cohesion shattered by the civil war, presents particular challenges requiring community consultation. Locally based organizations that meet perceived needs are more likely to be sustainable. For instance, one widely recognized need is affordable and adequate childcare, particularly for children of working parents. Local organizations for the care and support of both children and youth, run by women and men in the community, might, therefore, be an appropriate initiative that serves both an immediate need while also rebuilding local trust and social capital.

People living in poor urban communities recognize that in this post-conflict context the problem of violence is so complex that it requires cross-sector solutions. They also recognize that local ownership is crucial if the sense of fear, powerlessness, and lack of trust is to be overcome. Given the conventional sector divisions in government ministries and NGOs alike, developing such solutions is likely to prove challenging.

Annex A

Participatory Urban Appraisal Methodology

The techniques used in participatory urban appraisal usually involve focus-group discussions, but may also incorporate semistructured interviews, direct observation, ethnohistories and biographies, and case studies of individuals. These appraisal techniques can be conducted in two main ways: first, in local community centers or communal buildings; second, "in the street" within a community, which may involve discussions on street corners, beside football or basketball pitches, or outside people's houses.

The discussions with community members are based on a series of participatory urban appraisal tools that can elicit information on a range of issues. In the context of the current study, various tools were used to gather information on the following themes: community characteristics; the history of the community and violent events; general problems and types of violence as perceived by communities; poverty, well-being, and violence; changes over time in levels of violence, social capital, and exclusion; causes and consequences of different types of violence; social capital and mapping of social institutions; and, finally, strategies and solutions for dealing with and reducing violence (see Moser and McIlwaine 1999 for further details). Box A.1 provides a summary of the main types of tools used in the study.

Box A.1   Summary of main participatory urban appraisal tools on violence

Matrix of general data
Matrix of social organization
Listing of general problems
Ranking of general problems
    (scoring, "onion" diagram, or flow diagram)
Listing of types of violence
Ranking types of violence
    (scoring, "onion" diagram, or flow diagram)
Map of institutional relationships
Preference matrix on social institutions
Participatory map of the community
Participatory map of secure and insecure places
Matrix on history of the community
Matrix on trends of general problems
Matrix on trends of types of violence
Timeline—daily, weekly, monthly
Timeline—yearly
Timeline—long term (over period of a number of years)
Causal flow diagram on types of violence or other problems
Problem tree
Listing of strategies to cope with violence
Diagram of strategies to cope with violence
Listing of solutions to reduce violence
Diagram of solutions to reduce violence
Drawings

Source: Field notes of research teams.

Annex B

General Problems in Communities

Table B.1 Problems identified by community members (*percentage of all problems cited*)

Type of problem	Concepción, Guatemala City	Nuevo Horizonte, Guatemala City	La Merced, Guatemala City	San Jorge, Chinautla	Sacuma, Huehuetenango	Limoncito, San Marcos	El Carmen, Santa Lucía Cotzumalguapa	Villa Real, Esquipulas	Gucumatz, Santa Cruz del Quiché	All Communities
Violence	**54**	**51**	**46**	**33**	**60**	**49**	**47**	**36**	**51**	**48**
Theft	6	10	13	1	13	9	17	8	8	10
Gangs	11	6	9	13	11	12	6	5	6	9
Intrafamily violence	9	7	5	11	4	7	7	1	7	6
Drugs	6	10	6	3	8	6	3	6	6	6
Alcoholism	4	6	5	4	4	8	7	3	7	5
Fights, shootings	2	5	6	0	6	0	0	7	2	3
Rape	4	3	1	1	4	1	2	0	1	2
Killings	7	0	0	0	3	0	0	3	0	2
Kidnappings	3	1	0	0	2	0	4	0	2	1
Loitering	1	1	1	0	1	0	0	0	4	1
Prostitution	0	2	0	0	1	0	1	1	1	1
Danger	0	0	0	0	3	4	0	2	3	1
Human rights abuse	0	0	0	0	0	0	0	0	3	0
Physical capital problems	**19**	**21**	**33**	**13**	**15**	**39**	**34**	**26**	**32**	**26**
Lack of public services	8	14	17	6	8	20	12	17	17	13

(Table continues on next page.)

Table B.1 (continued)

Type of problem	Concepción, Guatemala City	Nuevo Horizonte, Guatemala City	La Merced, Guatemala City	San Jorge, Chinautla	Sacuma, Huehuetenango	Limoncito, San Marcos	El Carmen, Santa Lucía Cotzumalguapa	Villa Real, Esquipulas	Gucumatz, Santa Cruz del Quiché	All Communities
Poverty	4	3	7	1	1	6	11	1	4	4
Lack of transport	0	1	5	2	4	10	2	6	6	4
Unemployment	1	2	2	0	1	4	0	1	4	2
Housing	4	1	1	0	0	1	1	1	0	1
Work conditions	0	0	0	4	0	0	7	0	0	1
Human capital problems	**6**	**14**	**14**	**19**	**6**	**5**	**8**	**5**	**10**	**9**
Education	1	7	4	11	1	0	2	1	7	3
Health	1	1	4	3	5	4	3	1	1	3
Recreation	1	2	3	1	0	1	0	0	1	1
Family planning	1	2	0	0	0	0	2	1	0	1
Nutrition	0	1	1	1	0	1	1	0	1	0
Other services	0	2	3	0	0	0	0	2	0	1
Social capital problems	**9**	**9**	**4**	**16**	**12**	**7**	**12**	**10**	**6**	**10**
Lack of cooperation	7	5	2	6	3	6	4	8	1	5
Loss of traditions	0	1	0	6	3	0	4	1	0	2
Discrimination	2	0	1	1	2	1	3	0	0	1
Lack of police	0	3	0	0	3	1	0	0	0	1
Corruption	0	1	0	3	1	0	0	1	3	1
Natural capital	**12**	**6**	**3**	**18**	**7**	**0**	**0**	**22**	**1**	**8**
River	2	0	0	0	4	0	0	17	0	3
Environmental hazards	1	4	1	11	0	0	0	4	1	3
Pollution	9	2	2	7	3	0	0	0	0	2
Total	100	100	100	100	100	100	100	100	100	100

Source: 199 listings of problems by focus groups.

Annex C

Types of Violence

Table C.1 Types of economic, social, and political violence (*percentage of each type of violence within each community*)

Type of violence	Concepción, Guatemala City	Nuevo Horizonte, Guatemala City	La Merced, Guatemala City	San Jorge, Chinautla	Sacuma, Huehuetenango	Limoncito, San Marcos	El Carmen, Santa Lucía Cotzumalguapa	Villa Real, Esquipulas	Gucumatz, Santa Cruz del Quiché	Total
Economic	**44**	**39**	**58**	**21**	**48**	**59**	**52**	**40**	**55**	**46**
Drugs[a]	12	8	12	6	12	15	10	0	12	10
Insecurity	1	0	0	1	3	3	0	2	1	1
Robbery, assaults	11	11	12	4	5	18	22	6	18	12
Delinquency	3	7	3	0	3	5	2	1	5	3
Loitering	0	1	1	0	0	0	2	0	5	1
Maras (gangs)[b]	5	6	19	9	11	18	10	18	6	11
Prostitution	1	2	0	0	0	0	4	0	2	3
Kidnappings	3	2	1	0	11	0	0	2	6	3
Armed attacks	8	2	10	1	3	0	2	11	0	4
Social	**60**	**57**	**48**	**75**	**48**	**41**	**43**	**69**	**36**	**50**
Inside the home	16	13	8	29	6	15	15	9	11	14
Intrafamily violence	16	13	8	29	6	15	15	9	11	14

(Table continues on next page.)

Table C.1 *(continued)*

Type of violence	Concepción, Guatemala City	Nuevo Horizonte, Guatemala City	La Merced, Guatemala City	San Jorge, Chinautla	Sacuma, Huehuetenango	Limoncito, San Marcos	El Carmen, Santa Lucía Cotzumalguapa	Villa Real, Esquipulas	Gucumatz, Santa Cruz del Quiché	Total
Outside the home	23	35	20	35	30	26	15	44	20	28
Fights	15	20	2	23	18	21	2	18	5	14
Deaths	2	5	3	1	4	0	3	13	0	3
Alcoholism	5	6	11	7	7	5	7	11	10	8
Lynchings	0	0	1	0	0	0	1	2	0	1
Other[c]	1	4	3	4	1	0	2	0	5	2
Outside or inside the home	13	7	11	10	9		12	7	5	8
Rape	13	7	11	10	9	0	12	7	5	8
Political	**4**	**6**	**3**	**1**	**7**	**0**	**5**	**0**	**8**	**3**
Police abuses	1	1	2	1	1	0	1	0	4	1
Assassinations	2	2	0	0	3	0	0	0	3	1
Discrimination	1	0	1	0	1	0	0	0	0	0
Threats and terrorism	0	0	0	0	2	0	1	0	0	0
Human rights violations	0	3	0	0	0	0	3		1	1
Total	**100**	**100**	**100**	**100**	**100**	**100**	**100**	**100**	**100**	**100**

a. Drugs were classified as an economic form of violence due to their close link with theft and mugging.
b. Gangs were classified as an economic form of violence due to their close link with theft.
c. Includes *machismo*, presence of satanic cults and accidents.

Source: 154 listings of types of violence from focus groups.

Bibliography

Baulch, B. 1996. "Editorial—The New Poverty Agency: A Disputed Consensus." *IDS Bulletin* 27 (1):1–10.

CIEN (*Centro de Investigaciones Económicas Nacionales*). 1998. *La violencia en Guatemala: un tema prioritario. Carta Económica* 190 (October):1–8. Guatemala City.

Chambers, R. 1992. *Rural Appraisal: Rapid, Relaxed and Participatory.* IDS Discussion Paper 311. Brighton.

———. 1994a. "The Origins and Practice of Participatory Rural Appraisal." *World Development* 22 (7):953–69.

———. 1994b. "Participatory Rural Appraisal (PRA): Analysis of Experience." *World Development* 22 (9):1253–68.

———. 1994c. "Participatory Rural Appraisal (PRA): Challenges, Potentials and Paradigms." *World Development* 22 (10):1437–54.

Chambers, R. 1995. *Poverty and Livelihoods: Whose Reality Counts?* IDS Discussion Paper 347. Brighton.

CEH (Comisión para el Esclarecimiento Histórico). 1999. *Guatemala, Memory of Silence*, Guatemala: CEH.

De León, C. R. 1998. "El fenómeno de los linchaminetos y su relación con el tejido social comunitario antes de la firma de la paz." Paper presented in the Foro-Taller, Linchamminetos: Diagnóstico y búsqueda de soluciones. Panajachel, Guatemala, May.

Ferrigno F., V. 1998. "El estado democrático de derecho frente al conflicto social." Paper presented in the Foro-Taller, Linchamminetos: Diagnóstico y búsqueda de soluciones. Panajachel, Guatemala, May.

Groothaert, C. 1998. "Social Capital: The Missing Link?" Social Capital Initiative Working Paper 3. Washington D.C.: World Bank.

————. 1999. "Local Institutions and Service Delivery in Indonesia." Local Level Institutions Working Paper 5. Washington, D.C.: World Bank.

Harriss, J. and P. De Renzio. 1997. "An Introductory Bibliographic Essay. 'Missing Link' or Analytically Missing? The Concept of Social Capital." *Journal of International Development* 9 (7):919–37.

IEPADES (Instituto de Ensenanza para el Desarrollo Sostenible). 1998. "Seguridad ciudadana en Guatemala: diagnóstico de la problemática post-conflicto." Guatemala City. Processed.

Jonas, S. 2000. *Of Centaurs and Doves: Guatemala's Peace Process.* Boulder, Colo.: Westview Press.

Koonings, K. and L. Kruijt, eds. 1999. *Societies of Fear: The Legacy of Civil War, Violence and Terror in Latin America.* London: Zed Books.

MINUGUA (*Misión de Naciones Unidas de Verificación en Guatemala*). 1998a. *Third Report, Verification of Compliance with the Commitments Made in the Agreement on the Implementation, Compliance and Verification Timetable for the Peace Agreements.* New York: United Nations.

————. 1998b. *Second Report, Verification of Compliance with the Commitments Made in the Agreement on the Implementation, Compliance and Verification Timetable for the Peace Agreements.* New York: United Nations.

Moser, C. 1996. "Confronting Crisis: A Comparative Study of Household Responses to Poverty and Vulnerability in Four Urban Poor Communities." Environmentally Sustainable Studies and Monograph Series 8. Washington, D.C.: World Bank.

————.1998. "The Asset Vulnerability Framework: Reassessing Urban Poverty Reduction Strategies."*World Development* 26 (1):1–19.

Moser, C. and J. Holland. 1997. *Urban Poverty and Violence in Jamaica.* World Bank Latin American and Caribbean Studies Viewpoints. Washington D.C.: World Bank.

Moser, C. and C. McIlwaine. 1999. "Participatory Urban Appraisal and its Application for Research on Violence." *Environment and Urbanization* 11.

————. 2000. *Urban Poor Perceptions of Violence and Exclusion in Colombia.* Washington, D.C.: World Bank, Latin America and the Caribbean Region, Urban Peace Program.

Moser, C. and E. Shrader. 1999. "A Conceptual Framework for Violence Reduction." Sustainable Development Working Paper 2. Urban Peace Program Series. Washington, D.C.: World Bank.

Narayan, D. 1997. *Voices of the Poor: Poverty and Social Capital in Tanzania.* Environmentally and Socially Sustainable Development Studies and Monograph Series 20. Washington, D.C.: World Bank.

Narayan, D., C. Chambers, M. Shah, and P. Petesch. 1999. "Global Synthesis: Consultations with the Poor." Washington, D.C.: World Bank, Poverty Reduction and Economic Management Network, Poverty Group.

ODHAG (Oficina de Derechos Humanos del Arzobispado de Guatemala). 1998. *Informe Proyecto Interdiocesano de Recuperación de la Memoria Histórica (REMHI), Guatemala: Nunca Más.* Guatemala City: ODHA.

————. 1999. *Report of the Archdiocese Project Recuperation of Historical Memory (REMHI)* (international edition), *Guatemala: Never Again.* CIIR and LAB: London.

O'Kane, T. 1999. *Guatemala: A Guide to the People, Politics and Culture.* London: Latin American Bureau.

Palencia Prado, T. 1996. "Peace in the Making: Civil Groups in Guatemala." London: Catholic Institute of International Relations.

Palma, D. 1998. "La violencia delincuencial en Guatemala: un enfoque coyuntural." Guatemala City: Universidad Rafael Landívar. Processed.

PNUD (*Programa de las Naciones Unidas de Desarrollo*). 1998. *Guatemala: los contrastes del desarrollo humano.* PNUD: Guatemala City.

Ravaillon, M. 1992. "Poverty Comparisons: A Guide to Concepts and Measures." Living Standards Measurement Study Working Paper 64. Washington, D.C.: World Bank.

Rubio, M. 1997. "Perverse Social Capital: Some Evidence from Colombia." *Journal of Economic Issues* 31 (3):805–16.

Smith, C. 1990. *Guatemalan Indians and the State: 1540–1988,* Symposia on Latin America Series. Austin: University of Texas Press.

Uphoff, N. 1997. *Giving Theoretical and Operational Content to Social Capital.* Ithaca, N.Y.: Cornell University, Government Department. Processed.

Warren, K. B. 1998. *Indigenous Movements and their Critics: Pan-Maya Activism in Guatemala.* Princeton, N.J.: Princeton University Press.

Wilson, R. 1995. *The Maya Resurgence in Guatemala, Q'eqchi' Experiences.* Norman: Oklahoma University Press.

World Bank. 1995. *World Bank Participation Sourcebook.* Environment Department Papers. Washington, D.C.

————. 1998. "Violence in Colombia: Towards peace, partnerships and sustainable development." World Bank Sector Study. Washington, D.C. Processed.

————. 1999. *Violence in Colombia: Building Sustainable Peace and Social Capital.* Environmentally and Socially Sustainable Development Sector Management Unit Report 18652-CO. Washington, D.C.

BAKER & TAYLOR